Alaskan Adventures—Hunting and Fishing by Faith

BERT SCHULTZ

WESTBOW®
PRESS
A DIVISION OF THOMAS NELSON
& ZONDERVAN

WestBow Press books may be ordered through booksellers or by contacting:

WestBow Press
A Division of Thomas Nelson & Zondervan
1663 Liberty Drive
Bloomington, IN 47403
www.westbowpress.com
1 (866) 928-1240

ISBN: 978-1-4908-5609-4 (sc)
ISBN: 978-1-4908-5610-0 (hc)
ISBN: 978-1-4908-5608-7 (e)

Library of Congress Control Number: 2014918273

Printed in the United States of America.

WestBow Press rev. date: 11/05/2014

Thank you to the many friends and family who contributed to the writing of *Alaskan Adventures—Hunting and Fishing by Faith*. I began writing this book many years ago, but in 2004 a house fire destroyed the computer, manuscript, and photographs. To further complicate matters, serious medical problems hindered the completion.

I express my heartfelt thanks:

To my wife, Donna Schultz, for countless hours typing, editing, and helping prepare this manuscript.

To Joyce Baker Porte for editorial assistance and encouragement.

To Valerie Porte McKenney for editorial and formatting assistance.

To Annette Segura Schultz for retyping the manuscript from a battered, hand-corrected, and incomplete copy.

To Steve Schultz for resolving computer problems.

To Bob Hain for his pencil drawings of Old Harbor and hunting cabin.

To Fred Turcott for the Alaska sunset cover photo, other scenery and moose photos.

To my friends who provided old snapshots: Tim Hiner, Floyd McElveen, and Paul Weimer.

To Ben Fisher for the cover photo of Fuller Lake and brown bear photo.

I dedicate this book to my wife, Donna, my best friend and companion for over sixty years.

PROLOGUE

On Halloween Eve 1931, in Altoona, Pennsylvania, I came into this world with a loud cry, and my mother called me her *spook baby*. My real name was Bertis Alton, named after my mother's two brothers. As I grew older I was called Sonny, and not because I was extremely bright. When I became a teenager, I convinced everyone to call me Bert.

At birth I joined two sisters, Doris and Joanne, ages seven and three. My mother was an exceptional wife and mother. She had the gift of hospitality. When our church had a guest missionary or preacher, an invitation was extended to come to our home for dinner. God used these contacts to develop a desire for Christian ministry in our lives. When in third grade, I began lessons on the alto saxophone. Mom was musical and played piano. She directed my practice sessions and beat out the time on the dining room table. Her wonderful sense of humor was evident when she declared that she could have played the saxophone if she would have just learned to blow it. My ability to play and sing has been an asset to my ministry in churches and at Solid Rock Bible Camp.

My father, Otto, was full-blooded German, a good disciplinarian, and a hard worker. He worked for the Pennsylvania Railroad a couple of years as a plumber but felt it had no future with its periodic layoffs. He then managed a grocery store for a man who owned two.

His mother died when he was only three. His father and older sisters raised him till he was sixteen, when he left home for work. It was the middle of the Great Depression, and Altoona, being a railroad town, had its difficulties. Fortunately Dad always worked, even though the pay was low. He later went to work for C.W. Shaffer and Co., a local grocery store chain in Blair County.

We were raised in a Methodist church, and Dad was the superintendent of the Sunday school for all my growing up years. The Psalmist said in Psalm 139:13, 14 NIV "For you created my inmost being; you knit me together in my mother's womb. I praise you because I am fearfully and wonderfully made. Your works are wonderful, I know that full well." The Lord knew me before I was born and laid His hand upon me.

When I was ten years old, the second World War began, with all its sorrow and death. I remember hearing over KDKA in Pittsburgh that the United States had been attacked at Pearl Harbor, and President Roosevelt declared war on Japan.

The following summer an evangelist was invited to our church. Mr. Bonnie and his wife arrived for a week of meetings. Each day after school we met for a children's meeting. Jerry, a dummy, was the attraction. Mr. Bonnie, an excellent ventriloquist, said if we attended all week, Jerry the dummy would do something none of us kids could do. Yeah, right! I knew there were lots of things I could do that Jerry couldn't. Interest was high, and I just had to see this. So I went to all the meetings.

On Friday Jerry turned his head in a complete circle. I also tried. Mr. Bonnie said there was something we children could do that Jerry couldn't, and I listened carefully. We could have a relationship with God through His Son, Jesus Christ. Receiving Him as our Savior, we would have eternal life and go to heaven someday. Jerry could not do that. Mr. Bonnie went on to explain the Gospel fully, and I received the Lord Jesus as my Savior.

At the evening meetings the gospel was preached, and Mrs. Bonnie played the piano and sang beautifully. By the end of the week, about half of the congregation responded to the invitation and went forward to the altar, knelt, and received the Lord as Savior, including our pastor.

Within two weeks, those who rejected Christ wanted us out of the church. So we left and started the First Evangelical Methodist Church. We met in the Jaffa Mosque for a couple of years before we built our own church. The Lord was hunting for those who would believe in Him. He used Mr. Bonnie to fish for us through the Word of God. We were caught by the love of Christ.

A few years after the church was built, the congregation purchased an old farm outside Williamsburg, Pennsylvania, for a Bible camp. It was named Camp Manahath. I was now a young teen, and I looked forward to camp every summer. I worked on work crew. Once, when sweeping the dining hall, I hit the table leg with the broom and over went the table, and all the bowls of spaghetti slid to the floor. The cook ordered me out of the kitchen once and for all.

Our counselor was a young man about twenty. He was exhausted as the week progressed. Friday night he fell asleep early. We climbed out the upstairs window, slid down the porch post, and drove off to the Blue Hole. The older boys drove us.

The Blue Hole was an open pit ore mine. Springs gushing cool, blue water filled it suddenly. It was abandoned quickly, leaving behind equipment. It was deep and dangerous but refreshing and beautiful under the full moon. After a couple of hours we returned quietly to our bunks.

The camp wasn't much for facilities with only one house for a dorm, dining hall, kitchen, and a barn used for meetings. The milk shed became the snack shop. There was one horse to ride, and one canoe to paddle in the smelly, paper mill–polluted stream. In the meetings we were taught the Bible and learned about missions. We enjoyed craft classes and great campfire services. Just being away from the city, out in the country, was great for all of us.

The summer of my senior year, Reverend Burtner spoke for our teen camp. He directed Mount Lu San Bible Camp near Harrisburg, Pennsylvania, the state capital.

At our campfire service he spoke from Romans 6 and Romans 12 KJV and his topic was about counting ourselves dead to sin but alive unto Jesus Christ.

There was a family graveyard on the farm. Pastor Burtner said, "If we were to dig up one of those graves, we would only find bones. If you tried to talk to them, of course, you would get no answer. They are dead and give no response. We are to consider ourselves dead to the world and alive unto Jesus Christ. We are not to respond to the world and its allurement but only to Jesus Christ. He wants to direct our lives."

Romans 12:1–2 KJV: Present your bodies a living sacrifice, holy, acceptable unto God, which is your reasonable service.

At this point in life I didn't know what to do with my life. My dad wanted me to go into the antique business with him. My high school band buddies wanted me to join the Naval Reserve band. I was confused. So I said, "Lord, I am committing my life to you, now I am yours. You lead me, and I am going to wait till you show me what plan you have for my life."

That fall I was elected president of the Miracle Book Club. A group of about forty teens met for Bible study and fellowship in the George Noon home every Saturday night. Mr. Wilt, the leader, challenged us as we studied the Word of God. Christian service ministries involved our club members in street meetings, detention homes, and jail ministry. We learned to serve.

Living in the Bible belt, as Altoona was called, gave us opportunity to hear many missionaries. When they came through Altoona, Mr. Wilt would have them come and share their ministries. I was burdened for the whole world. A missionary came from Alaska. Louise Robinson told of her ministry among the Aleuts of Kodiak and the Alaska Peninsula. It was like a dart stuck in my heart, and I knew right then God wanted me in Alaska.

After graduation, I got a summer job with the city repairing and sweeping streets, and collecting garbage.

My cousin, Bill Briggs, and my future brother-in-law, Roy Hunter, were students at the Bible Institute of Pennsylvania. They encouraged me to apply. I had joined Calvary Baptist Church, and Pastor Ralph Stoll also urged me to attend. After prayer I applied and was accepted. I headed for Philadelphia in the fall of 1950. Much to my surprise, they couldn't find my name listed but soon found Bertis assigned to the girls' dorm. They corrected that in a hurry, and I roomed with Bill and Roy that first year. The second year we moved into the YMCA building, and Bible Institute of Pennsylvania and Philadelphia School of the Bible merged to become Philadelphia Bible Institute.

We had mission prayer groups, and I attended the North American group. I had a stack of prayer cards of Alaskan missionaries and prayed faithfully for each one. One day the leader of the group said to me, "Bert, there are a lot of students interested in Alaska. Why don't you break off and have your own prayer group?" I agreed and started the Alaska prayer group.

I dated a girl named Donna Porte. She was a member of Calvary Baptist Church in Altoona, which I had just joined. The last night at church before leaving for school, we were all asked to give our testimonies and tell where we were attending school. There were six going to Philadelphia. Afterward I was standing with my sister in the back of the church when Donna came by, and my sister said, "Oh Donna, you are going to Philadelphia where my brother is going. I will have him take care of you." We were both a little embarrassed.

Well, you guessed it. The Monday we started the Alaska prayer group, Donna was there. We compared notes on our next date, and I discovered God had called her to Alaska. After three years of dating and serving the Lord together on Christian service assignments and as youth pastor at Essington Baptist Church, we fell in love. Graduation was in June, and on August 22, 1953, we married.

After getting my degree at Wheaton College, we began deputation and support raising in the fall of 1955. We looked forward to beginning missionary service in Alaska. As I look back over my life, I can truly say how grateful I am for that decision God led me to make at Camp Manahath. *Lord, I commit my life to You, and I will wait for You to show me what You want to do with my life.* Truly He led every step of the way and proved more than faithful to His word. Mark 1:17 KJV. *Come ye after me and I will make you to become fishers of men.*

These fishing and hunting adventures are twofold. First, spiritual, as we ministered the Word of God, hunted for opportunities to be fully used by God, and saw Him establish His work and will in our lives. Then, the physical hunting and fishing, to see His faithfulness to provide all of our needs through my limited hunting and fishing skills.

Old Harbor nestled by the bay and mountains

CHAPTER 1

Kodiak Scare

My family and I came to Alaska in May 1957. Our destination: Old Harbor, an Aleut village on Kodiak Island, about as remote as you can get. Little did I know that only two months later I would have an adventure that would turn me into an old-timer in a hurry—a five-mile hike through terrain in my Sunday suit and carrying a suitcase with bear signs all around. And to top it off, a frightening skiff ride through heavy seas with fears of imminent disaster.

We flew to Kodiak Island after getting acquainted with the missionaries on the Kenai Peninsula. I was to work with missionary Dave Selden to build missionary housing in the village of Old Harbor, located on the southeast coast of Kodiak Island.

The single missionary, Violet Able, had been in the village for many years and wanted a family there to minister to the villagers. She lived in a small house that was inadequate for a family and sacrificed to provide money for a family home. Kadiak Fisheries brought all the materials for the house to Alaska on a fish tender.

We arrived in Kodiak and were met at the airport by Stan Alveen. We were stranded in Kodiak for a week because of poor weather. Kodiak Airways, via the Easter Egg, a seaplane, finally got us to Old Harbor.

It was a thrilling sight to see the village we had only seen in pictures. Now, after seven years preparing for missionary work in Alaska, we had arrived. Violet and the people graciously greeted us. We settled into a small house rented from brothers. The work began—hand digging the foundation and footings. The house walls began to go up.

About two months later, our Alaska field chairman flew to Kodiak and called a mission meeting in Kodiak. I put on my only good clothes, a dress suit, and then took a small suitcase and caught the next mail flight out. I arrived in Kodiak and found that Dale, Alaska field chairman, had Stan fly him down to the village about the same time I was traveling to Kodiak on Kodiak Airways. Stan was a bit disturbed over the confusion but agreed to fly me back to Old Harbor bright and early the next morning. We were on our way by 6:30 a.m. Stan lived on the water channel and kept his plane at his own dock.

The morning was clear for Kodiak, and we made good time, a distance of about sixty-five miles. We came over Old Harbor lagoon, and the tide was in and waves high. So we couldn't land. Stan buzzed the village to let them know we were in the area then flew across the Sitkalidak Straits to Nels Christiansen's Saltry. Nels was an elderly Norwegian who built a salting plant for herring during the sailing days. He put his whole life and savings into the saltry. Later the freezer ships came and fish were no longer salted. Nels still lived there in one of the cabins used by workers.

We couldn't land in his bay because the tide was in, and the fiercely blowing wind made it too dangerous. Now Stan flew back across to the village and buzzed them again and headed to Kaluda Bay northeast of the village. He flew high enough that I could see where we were going to land and see Nels's saltry.

"You see where you want to go about five miles to Nels's cabin from where I will let you out, at Kaluda Bay," Stan said.

We landed and pulled up to the beach, and I jumped out with my overnight suitcase. "Be sure to keep to the left or you will end up around the point of the bay and miss Nels's cabin. Stay to the left as you travel," he said and waved good-bye.

After stepping off the plane float to the beach, my adventure was just beginning. You wouldn't be able to imagine five miles through the terrain I was about to experience. I hadn't gone more than thirty yards when I came to a forest of small trees, about three to five inches in diameter about two feet apart. It was possible to maneuver through cautiously but would have been easier without a suitcase. It was good I was only twenty-five years old and in excellent physical condition. After about a half mile, there appeared hummocks or tufts of mossy grass with water around them. So now I had to pick my footing from clump to clump, swinging and swaying between the small trees, using them for pivots with one arm to maneuver my body forward.

This went on for about another half mile till I came onto higher ground and left the trees behind to find a game trail. It was unmistakable and well traveled, going around bends and up over hills and down. About the time I was feeling grateful for the good walking conditions, I realized that there were no moose on this trail. The Aleuts at Old Harbor said there were no brown bears over there. But I thought to myself, *They could be wrong, and I have a good four miles or so to go.* It was the driest summer the old timers had ever seen. The trail was dry and packed, and I didn't see any bear tracks. I came up over a knoll, and there to my right was a place smashed down in the deep grass where something had been lying. The grass was green in the bed.

I realized how fresh it must be, and perhaps the bear or bears were there overnight and had just left. Wow! I didn't want to walk over a hill and run into them, so I started to sing hymns and choruses as loud as I could, and I sang all the verses. I kept walking, looking, and singing for the next hour or so. Finally coming up one hill, I could see water ahead in the distance and the beach going off and around in an arc to the left and out of sight. I knew I must stay to the left and not get caught on the far right point of land and a dead end. The tide was still high enough to fill these low channels back in the depressions of the land. I would walk all the way around the end of them and then come to another going farther inland. I was getting exhausted, so I rolled up my suit pants and waded across the salt-water channels. Once or twice I was up to my waist in the water, and my progress was slowed. Finally after fifteen to twenty partial baptisms, I came to the rocky beach. When I say rocky, I mean rocky. The rocks were from baseball size to boulders the size of a chair, which made it difficult to walk. Later I began to see cabins in the distance.

I had been to Nels's place earlier in the summer to pick berries and have a picnic. My family, Vi, and a few villagers made the trip with me. I now came up off the beach and passed the first cabin on a nice trail. The last cabin had a broom, and a bucket outside the door, and smoke coming out the chimney. I politely knocked, and I heard a Norwegian voice say, "Come in."

When I opened the door, there was Nels Christiansen lying in bed with his head propped up in a reading position. "Vel, Bert, vat are you doing over here?" I told my story, and he said he heard an airplane fly over and wondered. I asked him if there were any brown bear in the area and described the trail I walked. His reply was, "You're a lucky boy, Bert. Yes, there are bears here. I know because I have lived here a long time. Now, get those wet clothes off and put on some dry ones."

He had just been to the city of Kodiak the day before and had brought back groceries and some delicious iced buns. They were warming on the stove. He poured me a cup of coffee, and we chatted about his saltry while my clothes dried. It was still blowing a bit, and the tide was still going out. After a look out the window, he said, "I'll take you across in the dory."

After a while the weather was suitable, and Nels gave me a raincoat and boots to put on over my dry clothes. We walked down to the beach, and he told me to sit in the bow with my back to the waves and facing him. He had an eight-foot rowboat with a seven horsepower motor, which he pronounced Even-rude. The tide was going out, so we had to go way around to the left to get past the rocks. As we rounded the point, the waves were rolling about two to three feet, breaking across my back and into the boat. The little craft would rise up in the back. The prop would be out of the water and give a roar of acceleration till we went down into the next trough. Coming up, the water would splash on my back and into the boat. My first thought was, *This thing is not going to float long*. Nels had a coffee can with the top cut out, and he dipped slowly. I thought, *If he's not worried, why be concerned? He's crossed this strait many times*. Except the villagers said, "When Nels dies, it will be by drowning crossing the strait."

We were now nearing the middle of this wide body of water when I saw a Kadiak Fisheries diesel boat coming. It was about twenty-two feet long with a cabin and fish hold. They were coming from a cabin across from the village, used by Fish and Game officers. That is where they thought I might have hiked. Dale had chartered the boat to come after me, but I wasn't there, of course. By now they spotted Nels and I bobbing up and down in the bay, and they came right toward us at a good pace. Within five minutes, they pulled up alongside and said, "Throw us the rope." I was already in the process when Nels said, "No, go on, go on," and the natives, knowing Nels, did just that as my heart sank. It took what seemed like an eternity getting to the shore of the village. There on the beach was Donna with tears in her eyes, holding onto our son, Scott. I gave hugs and kisses—and a big thanks to Nels for bringing me safely home.

We had our meeting to decide who was to stay as missionaries in Old Harbor and who would be led to minister elsewhere. But work remained to be completed before the end of summer.

By Fourth of July, we were ready to put the felt paper on the sheeting of the roof but took the day off to run the games and activities for the Fourth of July celebration. We had races of all kinds for both the guys and girls of each age group and a bike-decorating contest.

The big event started from the town path, crossed a field and up the grassy, green hill to the first bench and back. It was a sprint of about a half mile each way. A college student came to shore from a fish boat. He was excited about the race and the purse worth $25.00. He bragged about being a track star for UCLA and said he would win hands down. Seven Aleut boys lined up with him, and I blew the whistle for the start. He was first to the bottom of the mountain and gradually dropped to second, third, fourth place. When he reached the top, he was sitting down rubbing his cramped legs. He was all alone as the Aleut boys rolled down the grassy hill like cannon balls, stood up and shook themselves, and then ran for the finish line. That braggart was a while getting back and melted into the crowd.

Dave and I finished the house by early September, and Vi worked right along with us. Donna and I had been praying for guidance concerning our staying in Old Harbor. Dave and I both preached, and the women taught Sunday school. I could visit all 150 people in a short period of time. The village was very isolated. When the tide was in on the north end of the village, the lagoon cut off access. On the south end of the beach, the tide came into a rocky cliff. The price to fly just to Kodiak was ninety dollars. A plane or boat was the only way out.

Donna and Vi went by boat to the cannery to buy the winter's supply of food. Dave and I unloaded twenty-two barrels of diesel fuel for winter heat. Rolling them from the beach up to the house was exhausting work. Dave really adapted to everything in village life. He was from New England, loved boats, and knew how to build them. He loved the ocean and the secluded environment and seemed to work well with the people.

One day when Vi and Dave were on business about the house materials at the Kadiak Fishery, Donna and I were alone. The Easter Egg arrived. It was a purple, two-engine amphibian plane, a Grumman Goose, which landed in the water and, using wheels, pulled up on the beach. At the same time, a mother came to us very upset. Her son had been up on top of the school playground swings and fell directly on his head. His scalp was slit open all the way across but not a drop of blood. I knew he needed stitches; I washed it with green soap and wrapped it with gauze. With a towel wrapped around his head, I rushed him out to the plane that was ready to leave. I explained to the pilot that he needed to get this boy to the Kodiak hospital. He refused, saying he had passengers to go on down the Aleutian Chain. I insisted he turn around because the boy could die. He finally agreed and went back to Kodiak with the boy and his mother. The Lord was good in having the plane there at the right time, and a few weeks later the boy and mom returned to the village very grateful and on the mend.

In the village the missionary has many problems and crises to handle, besides ministering to spiritual needs. Dave seemed better equipped for village ministry. When the time came for the decision to be made as to who would stay and who would go on to another assignment, we knew we would leave the village. I felt very confined, and needed more space and different challenges. We moved to Sterling on the Kenai Peninsula, 140 miles south of Anchorage. I became the missionary pastor at Northland Baptist Church and with other missionaries founded Solid Rock Bible Camp. So the Alaskan adventure of missionary service began fifty-seven years ago.

CHAPTER 2

Hunting Moose

We arrived in Sterling, Alaska, on the Kenai Peninsula in the fall of 1957 to serve as missionaries at Northland Baptist Church. It was located on the corner of Robinson Loop Road and Sterling Highway, the entrance to Swanson River country and the newly discovered oil field. Sterling became our Alaska home for the next three years. Paul Weimer, the outgoing pastor, had left in September for special missionary assignment in the *lower forty-eight*. He had bagged his moose before he left and had it in a freezer at the Pederson's store and post office. They had a generator. He graciously gave it to us for our winter meat.

Now over a year had gone by, and I was eligible for a resident hunting license and anxiously awaited the perfect time. In the late fifties, there was an early season in August and a late season in November. We called this *the homesteader's season*, when it was cold enough to hang your moose in a shed and cut off a piece, as you needed it. In the late season the moose would come down out of the Kenai Mountains when the snow got deep and move across the flats toward the Kenai River. That November they were coming through our area, crossing the Robinson Loop Road and Sterling Highway, and foraging around till the Kenai River would freeze over and then cross to the Funny River country for the winter.

We had prayed one morning that God would provide a moose for our family needs. I drove my station wagon very slowly around the Loop Road. I saw many tracks but no moose in sight. I went back home for breakfast. Scott, almost three, said, "Daddy, I pray for moose." I went out again and drove the same route and noticed large fresh tracks had crossed the road since I had gone for breakfast. I parked the station wagon and followed the tracks up along the bank and down to the left. After walking some distance, there was an open area about seventy yards ahead, and a big bull moose was slowly walking into full view. I held my breath, clicked off the safety on my 30-06, and fired into his hump. He reared up on his hind legs and then fell to the ground. I cautiously walked up to him and made sure he was dead.

I took a minute to thank the Lord for answered prayers and began to dress out the moose with the tools I had in my pack. I helped several homesteaders butcher their moose and pack them out, so I had some experience. When the bull fell, he landed with his back against a tree, which made it difficult for butchering. I opened him up to let him cool and walked about a quarter mile to a homesteader's home. He had a small dozer and pulled the moose out to his cabin. We finished butchering it into six pieces and loaded it into my station wagon. I headed home. I later gave him some meat for his help.

I arrived home all bloody. Scott shouted, "Daddy got a moose, Daddy got a moose."

CHAPTER 3

Homer Trip

In the fall of 1959, my coworker Paul invited me to go hunting with him and Frank Wise, a resident and friend from Homer, Alaska.

Frank had a farm tractor especially rigged for hunting. It had large tires and middle idler wheels that assisted the tracks that went around the rear wheels. It also had a wooden box built on the back, which he used to haul coal off the beach for his homestead stove. A big game guide hired Frank to haul moose from the kill site to a bush airstrip to be flown out with the hunter.

Frank made a deal with the guide to fly us into the airstrip and later bring our moose out as a trade for hauling his clients' moose. Frank had the worst job. He had to drive the tractor twenty miles into the back country of the Caribou Hills through swamps and brush.

Paul and I drove to Homer and were flown in from the Homer airport to the bush strip. Frank met us there after leaving a day or two before us. We loaded our gear into the box on the back of the tractor and proceeded down off the ridge and through forests, swamps, and tundra, and over hills for an additional five miles from the air strip to virgin country.

Frank knew where he was going and stopped in a low draw that had a flowing creek. Here we set up camp, climbed to the top of the ridge, and picked out a large spruce tree. Frank climbed up the tree, trimming branches and making a place for us to stand. It was now late afternoon, and Frank motioned for us to climb up to him. We looked and he pointed out seven bull moose within a quarter mile of the tree. They were all sizes. I was strictly a meat hunter and didn't need a large moose for the three in my family. Across the first dip was a moose that had a small palm.

I told them that was fine for me. I climbed down out of the tree, and got my gun and pack. Quietly I circled around in the direction of the moose that was feeding and moving slowly. From the other ridge, I could see Frank and Paul up in the tree motioning for me to go left, and then they motioned to come forward slowly. It was a thick willow patch, but he was so busy feeding and pulling on the branches, he didn't know I was there. I saw the branches moving, and waited till I saw his rack, head, and neck. I quietly put a shell into the chamber, clicked off the safety, held my breath, and squeezed off the trigger with the scope hairs on his neck and skull base. Down he went.

My buddies were there in ten minutes with the tractor. After butchering, we went back to camp and hung moose #1 on a rack built from a pole hung between trees. It was now time to cook some supper and relax until bedtime.

We planned to get one moose each day and not rush our trip. Frank did have to leave Paul and me for half a day to haul moose to the airstrip for the guide and his hunters.

The next morning we were walking across the ridge to our tree, glassing with the binoculars, when Frank spotted a movement in the grass down at the bottom of the ridge to the left. Our mouths dropped open when we realized it was the gigantic rack of a bull moose lying down in the grass resting. He would raise his head up to look around periodically and then put his head down. He was a good one hundred twenty-five yards away, lying just in front of a clump of thick trees. We estimated his rack at six feet.

We planned our strategy because if Frank was seen or heard on his stalking, it would be one jump and Mr. Bull Moose would be in the thick woods and gone. There was a game trail down along the alder patch that would give cover to Frank for about fifty yards, and then he would be pretty much in the open.

Paul and I lay down on the ridge, sighted in on the moose. Frank was to take the first shot, and if the bull started for the woods and wasn't downed by his shot, we were to fire. The bull heard Frank and jumped up. Frank shot and the bull headed for the woods as Paul and I shot to stop him. The bull staggered and fell about thirty to forty feet inside the woods.

We all ran down the hill hoping he was wounded enough to be down. Paul and Frank went in the woods after the moose, and I circled around to the right. They yelled, "There he is," pointing down between where they were standing and me. I ran up to look, and the moose was not dead. I must have spooked him as I approached, and he flung his hind leg straight out toward me. I flung myself backward to the ground in surprise. His hoof missed my head by what I estimated at about twelve inches. His bloodshot eyes stared at us for a moment as Frank put him to rest.

As hunters always say, "Then starts the work." It took all three of us to turn him on his back, spread his legs, and begin to dress him. I never could figure out that expression. It should be *undress* him because he loses all his entrails and his hide in the process. Frank left to get the tractor, and Paul and I kept working on the bull. He was back about a half hour later to help finish up the butchering and load the moose and the seventy-two-inch rack into the tractor box. That was the close of day two.

The next morning from the spruce treetop, we spotted a nice four-year-old bull with a forty-two inch rack. He was about a quarter mile away. Paul did a great job of stalking, and within an hour, we heard shots, and Paul filled his moose ticket. Now the job began getting the meat, gear, and us to the airstrip.

The weather had been cool. The meat was in muslin bags and in good shape. We made it safely back to the Homer Airport, loaded the station wagon, and headed home.

The fellowship on a hunting trip, working together, enjoying the campfire and the stories, are the experiences you never forget. The Lord provided again. He is faithful.

CHAPTER 4

Bear Tales

The full basement at the Sterling parsonage collapsed because it was back-filled with blue clay instead of gravel. The house needed to be moved over onto a gravel pad. Paul had the area dug out and gravel hauled in to make a pad for the house. When we came to Sterling from Old Harbor, the house was ready to move. We put pipe under the beams to roll the house over closer to the church. Large 6x12 planks were put on the gravel pad to set the house on. We forgot to tell the women we were ready to move the house, and as the house was pushed, they came jumping and screaming out the door. They thought it was an earthquake. After moving the house, it was a little out of square with the church. A plank was put under the kitchen window, and I used hand motions to tell the D-7 Cat operator when to push and when to stop. When I put siding on the church the next fall, it lined up perfectly with the house siding.

Kermit Dowse attended the church and was a partner in a sawmill in North Kenai. I helped at the mill in exchange for spruce siding for the church and to build a classroom joining the church to the house.

I had been working at the sawmill two or three days a week, and we would sleep in a cabin that had thick plastic with fiber cords covering the window. We arrived one Monday and noticed the plastic had bear claw marks through the plastic. The next plastic window was torn out. The bear came in the cabin, crawled right across my bed, and rummaged through all the cupboards and counters. Everything was torn up and scattered. It took a half day to clean up the mess, but we knew he would be back. We put all the spoils into the garbage barrel by the lane. Sure enough, he was back the next evening rolling the barrel. Kermit got his rifle, went out the side door of the cabin very cautiously, waited for the bear to be in a good position, and *bang, bang*, down he went. We dressed him out, and he smelled good enough to eat. He had not been eating fish, only greens and occasional garbage. Nestor and Kermit said I could have the bear for meat, so I loaded my 1957 Plymouth station wagon and went home. Donna didn't like the looks of that bear hanging up. He was a nice six-footer, and the meat tasted a little like pork. It was nice to have more than moose meat for a change.

The old log Sterling schoolhouse still stands across Robinson Loop Road from the church. It was built before we arrived in 1957. The teacher, Mr. Bartell, was away for about two months, and I was asked to substitute teach seventeen kids in first to eight grades. I knew them well since most attended our Sunday school or youth group. I took my saxophone to school, and we sang Gospel choruses in music class.

The next teacher was Dan Rempel, who told me this funny bear story. Dan and his family were driving toward Cooper Landing. They had crossed the flat lands, over the mountains, and were going around the corner with Engineers Lake on the right. The car ahead stopped, and a large brown bear crossed in front of the car and moved down the bank on the lakeside. Dan pulled up behind to watch. The driver in front blew his horn, and a few minutes later the bear came up the bank, stepped over the guardrail cable, and stood up on his hindquarters. He slammed down with his forepaws, caving in the hood of the car. The bear got down on all fours and moved into the brush. That will teach you not to blow your horn at a brown bear. Sorry, no pictures to prove it, only an honest school teacher who told the story at church.

CHAPTER 5

A Lost Moose

The very next year Paul and I were invited again for the same kind of hunt. How could anyone refuse such a great offer in such beautiful country with such magnificent scenery and hunting? Just as the previous year, we were to fly in with the guide, and Frank drove the cleated tractor in the twenty-five to thirty miles to the airstrip.

The Lord had other plans, as you will see. We loaded up my station wagon for the trip to Homer with all our hunting gear and food. As we were winding our way out of Soldotna on the gravel road south, we came up to the top of the hill, and to our surprise two bull moose came down off the cut to the left in front of our vehicle and up the bank on the right of the road.

Flabbergasted and stunned, we stopped in a moment of confusion. Should we go after them or let them go? Why ruin a good hunting trip in the Caribou Hills? But why travel so far when meat is so close. Paul said he didn't really have time to go to Homer with the construction of the Soldotna church in progress. So we both got out and started up the bank.

15

At the top we looked, and there stood both bulls about thirty yards away looking at us. We confirmed which one we were to shoot, and Paul shot first. His bull shuddered but didn't go down.

My bull was too close to shoot because through the scope all I could see was hair. I quickly bumped the scope aside on its pivot mount and took aim. But the bull was behind a tree and moving away between more and more trees. I moved in his direction, but he gave me the slip. Paul and I hunted for about two hours circling around between a large swamp and more hills, knolls, and trees. He came upon his wounded moose still on his feet and made the killing shot.

I never found the other bull, so now I had to go to Homer alone without my hunting partner. It was a ninety-mile drive to Frank's homestead. A friend of Frank's was already in line to take Paul's place, and like the previous year, we flew into the bush airstrip from the Homer airport with all our gear. From the strip we loaded up our gear and ourselves into the coal box on the back of the tractor, and off we went through brush, across swamps, getting stuck but not for long, as Frank knew how to maneuver the rig. We reached our camp and were set up in a few hours.

Like the previous year, we planned one moose kill each day, return to camp, hang it on the cross pole, and enjoy the campfire food. There were the usual discussions of the day and more hunting stories and praise for God's provision.

Frank got his bull the next morning, and Ivan Auten, Paul's stand-in, got his the next day. Both were shot within a mile of our camp. The third day was the last day of hunting season. We arose to a thick fog that was still hanging low at 10:00 a.m., and the wind was blowing up on top of the ridges. Frank said that the moose would be lying low in the thickets and not moving much because the noisy wind in the trees made it hard for them to detect danger. We were to break up and pothole hunt and try to kick one out into the open.

I was a bit discouraged because of the conditions, but the Lord had always provided for my need of meat to feed my family. I knew He would be faithful.

I walked along a moose trail, not able to see more than thirty to forty feet. The fog was thick. I silently prayed, "Lord, I know you have a moose for me, but in this fog you are going to have to walk him up to me." I thought after this incident about Romans 8:26 KJV—The Spirit helps our infirmities for we know not how to pray as we ought: but the Spirit Himself makes intercession for us.

Well, the Lord knew my need, heard my prayer, and even led in my prayer. Just a few minutes later, as I was going up the steep trail, with hands literally on the slope in front of me, with my shoes digging in behind me, I reached the top. I was slowly getting to an upright position when I looked up the trail ahead, and there trotting toward me was a three-year-old bull moose. When he saw me, he put his front hoofs ahead and slid to a stop about twenty-five feet away.

We so surprised each other that for an instant neither of us knew what to do. I pulled my gun off my shoulder, kicked off the safety, and yelled at him because he was too close for my scope. He turned around and started to run back the way he had come, and I shot him behind the ear at about fifty feet. Down he went. I got down on my knees and thanked the Lord for his wonderful answer to prayer.

This was the beginning of an unusual moose retrieval. I gutted him out and propped his rib cage open with sticks to let him cool and headed back to camp. I had meandered all around in the fog, and I had difficulty getting reoriented. After a while I came across Frank after calling periodically. He wanted to see the moose site in order to plan how to get there with the tractor. I led him back to where I thought the moose had dropped. The more I looked and turned, the more confused I became. We looked till it was dark and went back to camp.

The next morning the guide flew over to tell Frank he had moose to haul to the airstrip. He cut the engine to quiet and yelled down that a moose was down and pointed. We ran in the direction he signaled, and he kept swooping down over the moose kill and would fly around again till we got close enough to spot it.

We waved and he flew off. The weather had been warm and fortunately I propped the carcass open, so it cooled pretty well that night. Frank went for the tractor, and I quartered the moose till he got back. We loaded him in the tractor box and hung him on the pole rack when we arrived at camp. Frank went to the airstrip to haul the guide's moose out to the strip for transportation to Homer.

I was talking to Frank during my writing of this story to clarify a few things, and he told me that one season in the early sixties he hauled forty-five moose to that airstrip. We talked about how few are taken now compare to back then.

Our hunting trip ended, and the following day after several flights, all our gear and moose were delivered to the Homer airport. I put my moose in the station wagon, and with grateful thanks and farewells, headed back to Sterling. We usually hang game for seven to ten days to cure and tenderize before butchering. That wasn't done that year because it was so warm, barely cooling to forty-five degrees at night.

CHAPTER 6

A Bear and Earthquake

In the early sixties, Bud Lofstedt helped missionaries get their meat for winter with his two-place plane on floats. He offered to take me out for a moose and told me where to meet him. We got an early start and took off out over the Kenai Flats, a myriad of knolls, lakes, and swamps. Minnesota brags of having 10,000 lakes. I think we have that many just on the Kenai Peninsula, not to mention all of Alaska.

Early in the morning, we spotted several moose by a lake drinking or in the bog at the lake's edge munching on greens. It's a dizzying experience, circling around and around, each spotting on his own side of the plane. We would see more cows than bulls. Suddenly Bud spotted a bull coming up the bank from the lake. The moose stopped on a sparely-treed area about two hundred yards from the lake. He landed and taxied as quietly as possible to the bank to let me get out and off the float. He would wait to see if I downed the moose, and if not he would take flight and try to spot it and show me where it had gone.

I crawled up the bank cautiously and made my way toward where the moose was seen from the air. He was standing there looking straight at me, the length of a football field, and that would be close. There was a problem. Between me and the moose was a tree that revealed half on one side and half on the other. I propped the gun over a downed tree to shoot, trying to miss the edge of the tree and hit the moose, with my vertical crosshair just right of the tree. He flinched but didn't go down. My 180-grain bullet didn't hit enough moose. He turned around and ran straight ahead through scattered trees and low brush. I walked slowly ahead for about five minutes looking left and right and straight ahead. Bud knew by now I didn't get the moose down, and I heard him start his engine and take off. I stopped next to some tall grass as Bud came over and began to circle. He put his wing right over me and circled showing me the general location.

I couldn't see the moose until the roar of his engine shocked the moose, and he jumped up not ten feet from me. He was running directly away from me. I pulled up and shot him at the base of his head, and down he went. Another shot was not necessary and he never moved.

Bud flew over again and flew out in the direction I was to pack the moose. He told me that often until you got the moose down, one is closer to another lake. So he would point by flight which direction to go. While I was butchering the moose, he would go back and get another hunter. When I had packed the moose out, he came back to pick me up.

Then the work began, and I got him gutted and cut in six pieces. I didn't have a tape, so I estimated his rack to be forty-eight to fifty-two inches, and at about four years old, not too tough to eat. I placed the meat against a log on a piece of plastic and covered it.

I tied a hindquarter on the pack board, and I hoisted the pack off the log. As I was turning it around to get my arm through the other loop and onto my shoulder, I staggered under the weight. Then I realized it weighed about 120 pounds. I also left my rifle under the plastic, and of course the moose head with rack still attached next to the meat. I began my trip to the lakeshore. I sat down exhausted to rest while I waited for Bud. I didn't have to wait long. Within an hour Bud was back and saw me. The shore was shallow and mushy. He came in as close as he could, and I waded out to him. Standing on the float, he swung my pack in behind the back seat, relieving my aching back. After discussion and laughter on how close the moose was to me in the grass, I got buckled in and we took off. Being a two-place plane, I was in the back seat for the return flight to Kenai.

About halfway on a twenty-minute flight, the isinglass top of the windshield began to flutter. Several screws popped out of the metal trim, and the roof shield was coming loose. I reached up to hold it down, but my hands were freezing. Bud handed me gloves that I put on one at a time, trying to hold the top together. The sun was glaring right in our eyes, and I didn't know how he could see. Bud said, "Hang on, we're going straight in." If the isinglass had gone out, we would have possibly blown the top off. But we made it.

Bud told me to be back the next morning at seven, and I could help his buddy put aluminum back in the place of the isinglass. I took my quarter moose home and hung it up to cure. Over supper I told the first half of this story.

The next day I was back at the lake, and the mechanic had just arrived. He cut the aluminum to size and drilled the holes to match the trim that came loose the previous day. He held and I screwed the sheet metal screws into place. We were about finished when Bud arrived at eight, bringing a plumber friend's wife along. Her husband couldn't get off work to hunt, so she was going to get the moose. With a two-place plane and no baggage, we were not overloaded. She sat between my legs and we put the seat belt around both of us.

We got off from the lake without a problem and headed out to my moose. To this day I don't know how those bush pilots know one lake from another. They fly so much, I guess they know them like the back of your hand. Well, we flew directly to the lake, and Bud circled around to point out the moose. We circled to see if everything was all right. The moose was still stacked and the plastic was over the top. But my mouth dropped open because the head with horns attached was gone. That could only mean one thing. A big brown bear had carried off the head and rack for a feast. He may not have taken it far, and my gun was there at the moose kill and not with me.

We landed, and Bud said to be careful.

"Thanks," I replied and got out and waded to terra firma. The pack-out with the first quarter the day before was about 120 pounds. I walked back the way I came, through some spruce trees to the big tree where a log went across a small creek and stopped. Across the creek was the tall grass I had to go through, and beyond was the moose kill. I read many stories about bears, and besides getting between the mother and her cubs, the next danger is taking the food they have discovered. But I also read the Bible many times and my life verse is Proverbs 3:5 and 6 KJV Trust in the Lord with all your heart and lean not unto your own understanding. In all your ways acknowledge Him and He shall direct your path.

What a promise. I decided to trust the Lord and go.

I started across the log with my pack on my back, still aware that brownie could be hiding in the grass and with one swing could knock my head off my shoulders. Another four yards and I stopped to listen if I could hear any sounds of munching, etc. It was quiet, so I moved on to my kill, grabbed my rifle from under the plastic, and chambered a shell. My moose kill was right next to a thick clump of small birch trees, and I could see a place where the bear might have dragged the moose head. I went quietly in that direction but not more than twenty-five or thirty steps to stop and listen. Since I didn't hear anything, I went back, laid the second hind quarter on the pack board, and in record time I had it tied down and on my back, and away I went.

Just as I got almost to the hummocks or moss tufts, I turned my ankle and down I went. It was so bad I wondered how I would put any weight on it, let alone pack out four more pieces of moose. Before making the second trip, I built a raft of small trees from deadfall and floated it on top of the muskeg and water. My plan was to stack the moose meat on the raft, so when Bud came back I would have it close to the plane. I got to my feet and hopped mostly on one foot, swinging the moose pack back and forth from pack to pack leg, walking it like a folded up metal chair. I worked the pack out to the raft site, flopped it down, and rested.

My ankle was swelling, but with my partial weight on it, the needle feeling wasn't as bad. I untied the pack from the meat and laid it next to my gun. It was time for another talk with the Lord. So I said, "Lord, I am going to walk away from my gun and look back at it laying there. If you give me perfect peace, I will know you will protect me from the bear." To pack moose and carrying the gun was difficult, especially now with a bum ankle. So I walked about twenty paces, stopped, and looked back at my gun, and the most unusual feeling of peace, rest, and assurance came over my whole being that I said, "Thank you, Lord," and went on.

I got all the way back to the big tree and the log over the creek and stopped. There was the high grass I had to go through without a gun. Oh, how Satan likes to bring doubts to your heart. So I said, "I'm trusting you, Lord," and went on. I got back to the moose, slapped a front shoulder on the pack board, and limped back to the float. I untied it and started back for piece four. I packed the fourth leg, went back for the last pack, and returned with all my moose meat safely on the float. I sat down on the game trail that goes all the way around almost every lake and cleared a place to build a small fire to warm myself. I broke off some dead twigs from the big spruce tree lying across the path and got a fire started.

As I was sitting on the tree, relaxing with the little fire beginning to give off some heat, that huge tree started to shake vigorously. I jumped up, startled with one thought on my mind. That brown bear must be on the other end. Anxiously peering down the log, I was relieved that the brownie was not on the other end.

It was an Alaskan earthquake, which lasted less than thirty seconds. I was glad to hear the drone of a plane in the distance, and I knew it was probably Bud. It was starting to spit rain, and I wanted my meat and me out of there.

Bud landed, pulled up close to my float, and said, "I see the bear didn't get you." I asked how he did with the other hunter. They saw a bull swimming across the lake, waited till it stepped on the beach, and she shot it. What an easy pack! That sure makes an easy story to tell when mine has taken several pages.

CHAPTER 7

A Trip to Paxson

One of the pastors I became acquainted with in the Kenai Peninsula Fellowship was a missionary from Cooper Landing, Reverend Floyd McElveen. We called him Brother Mac. He and Virginia had three sons and a daughter. Mac was a great fisherman, and he also loved to hunt. He had to do both to help support his family. Neither of us had Sunday night church services, so we would drive to Cooper Landing and meet with his family and a few others for fellowship on Sunday evening.

When we went hunting, we would leave Sunday night after the fellowship. We had to be back for prayer service on Wednesday evening. In late August, the caribou would cross the Denali Highway from the north side to the south side. We would drive all night to Paxson, then onto the gravel Denali Highway for about seventy miles. On this trip we took Jerry Hobart along, a Christian friend and hunter. We had Brother Mac's 1958 Chevy station wagon that had a roof rack to haul needed items. We were only about ten miles from Paxson when six or seven caribou of all sizes came down over the bank from our right, trotted across in front of our car, and went up on top of the bank to the left. They stood there for a moment looking down at us. Well, Mac was out of the car with his rifle, which he had right beside him, ready to shoot.

Jerry and I told him to wait till we got our rifles out of the back. With the back seat folded down, the rifles had shaken down between the seats and were lodged there. Mac was yelling to come, and we were yelling to wait. By now the caribou had started off across the open treeless tundra. We got to the top of the bank, and they had already covered half a mile— too far away to shoot. Actually, Mac couldn't shoot because you have to be off the road and across the bar ditch before shooting. After a discussion about our preparedness and disappointment, we agreed there would be more caribou ahead.

We drove another fifty miles, saw an old cabin down off the road, and decided to stop and check it out. We found out later it was an old Highway Department cabin used many years before. The door was half off the hinges. The bottom logs had rotted out, so the cabin had sunk a few feet and you needed to duck to get inside. An old, rusty stove stood in a corner, and there were three bunks made of logs. The roof was without a sky view, so we praised the Lord for a good shelter and made ourselves at home. We had a few more hours to hunt before dark. So we cooked up some food and took a short nap. This was before air mattresses, which would have made these saplings smoother.

Refreshed, we again started our hunt. You could see the caribou coming from a distance as we drove slowly. The biggest bull would be in the lead. If he saw danger ahead, he would turn back and move to another low draw in the road bank and make another approach with the other bulls following. There are a lot of small knolls and hills along the highway. They would make a dash for cover through a low spot to cross on a dead run. We noticed that they would usually turn back twice, but on the third attempt the big bull would lead them on and not turn back.

We were observing them getting closer and closer to the road and knew they were about to make the break. Suddenly a guy in a pickup came roaring around us to get the lead. He was going too fast and went beyond where they crossed. Mac stopped short of their crossing, which brought them across in front of us.

I jumped out and yelled to Jerry, "I'll take the first, you take the other." I jumped across the bar ditch, held my breath, and shot at about 100 to 120 feet. Down went the big bull. Jerry got his. But there were a group of army boys coming the other way. They were on top of a hill ahead of us, shooting down toward us.

I ran over to the caribou I had shot dead and laid down partly on him and yelled this one is mine. Mac and Jerry laughed at me, but they didn't realize this was the first big caribou I had ever shot. My dad only took me rabbit hunting in Pennsylvania, and up until now I had not even shot a deer in Pennsylvania.

We dressed out our caribou, loaded up the station wagon with the horns on top, and proceeded to hunt until it got too dark. Our hunt ended at nine due to exhaustion and lack of sleep. We headed back to our cabin, hung up the two caribou, had a snack and, with a thankful prayer time, went to sleep. Hunting in Alaska, even in the fall, means a very early rise. By five, ready or not, it was time to get up and have breakfast. Jerry was the chief cook, and we had pancakes, eggs, and bacon after the stove got hot enough.

The night before the pots got washed with dish drops but must not have been rinsed properly. We paid for that blunder. After driving for twenty miles, I yelled for Mac to stop, and Jerry and I both headed for the bushes.

You guessed it; we both had a bad case of the runs. I still can't figure out how Mac missed it completely. This went on all morning till we approached the only lodge on the Denali. Mac took a picture of the orange outhouse behind the lodge and one of us making a beeline toward it.

Things got better after a cup of coffee or two in the lodge. We decided to head on down the old Denali Highway to spot more caribou. We were allowed two each, so we had a few more to shoot. After traveling maybe an hour, caribou crossed ahead of us. We stopped and jumped out, crashing a shell in the chamber. There were seven to eight caribou in that group, and no other hunters were around. Mac and Jerry took off to the right and started shooting. The group got confused and meandered in among some small trees. A caribou came out through to my side. So I shot twice and he went down, but he was trying to get up and I had no more shells. I was calling for more shells to Mac and Jerry, but they had their hands full.

Mac shot two large caribou. He called the big one Rosco. My caribou was a young bull, probably a three-year-old with a much smaller rack. I ran up to where he was lying and struggling to get up. I got out my knife, pulled his head back, and slit his throat.

We talked about it later, how funny I would have looked if he had gotten up with me on his back. Crazier yet is how sometimes you do things on the spur of the moment in desperation that could be disastrous. That was my second caribou, Jerry had his second, and Mac got his two. That filled the station wagon, and we got our limit. We were headed for camp at mile post 84, but with permission hung the caribou up at the hunting lodge to let them cool. We planned to pick them up the next day on the way out.

We were tired, exhausted, and very sleepy, as we were to soon find out. We got in the station wagon with the racks tied on top and started for our cabin. All three of us were sitting in the front seat, and the sun was warm shining in the side window. Jerry fell asleep within a few miles, Mac was bobbing, and I was fighting sleep. I told Mac I would stay awake and keep him awake. The next thing I knew we were off the road on the left side, bumping up the bar ditch over rocks and bumps. We all jumped up as Mac hit the brakes and stopped in front of a boulder that was just a bit higher than the car hood. Five more feet and that would have been all she wrote. The Lord again proved His faithfulness in spite of our stupidity. We were able to get back up on the road and checked out under the station wagon, amazed there were no leaks and no flats, but we were wide awake; we made it back to the cabin.

That cabin didn't look that good now that we had our caribou. We decided to leave after packing up the gear and the two caribou we had hanging there. The plan was to try to sleep one at a time and take turns driving. Mac said he wanted to get home in time for prayer meeting, which would be a nonstop trip to Cooper Landing. We had burgers, fries, and coffee at the lodge, which was the first food since five o'clock breakfast. Jerry and I had lost that long ago, and we were beginning to feel like eating again.

After we ate, we had some rearranging to do to get all that meat put in gauze bags and stacked behind the front seat. The wagon was full all the way to the ceiling and to the back door with room for our gear and guns on top. The antlers were a sight to behold on top of the car, and turned a lot of heads on our trip home.

I took over the driving from Paxson to Glennallen. Jerry drove to Gun Site Mountain where we got gas, and Mac drove to Palmer. It was my turn again, and I drove from Palmer to Anchorage. The guys wanted to stop at a soft ice cream store along the road and kept hollering for me to stop, so I did. They got out to get the ice cream, and I was delirious. I was hollering to stop the car. I was pumping the brakes because even sitting still, the highway white stripe appeared to be going by very fast. They got me settled down, and I was relieved from driving. I have trouble sleeping in a moving vehicle; when I totaled up my sleep time, it amounted to about seven hours since Sunday morning.

We loaded our meat and horns into our own rigs at Mac's cabin, bid farewell, and headed on down the Peninsula. We had plenty of meat to enjoy for the winter, and again I greeted a happy family who was overjoyed to see me home safely with game.

CHAPTER 8

Hunting in Deep Freeze Temperatures

In the spring of 1961 we arrived back from missionary furlough and began to direct the ministry of Solid Rock Bible Camp. We built our home on the campground between regular scheduled camps, and Lee Van Sickle, a few others, and I dug the footings. The foundation was framed for concrete, and Elmer Banta from Ninilchik brought his big mixer for the pour. The house was closed in and usable by November, and I spent the next several years totally finishing it, as money was available.

My brother-in-law, Vince Porte, and his family had moved to Kenai as interim missionaries at Kenai Bible Church. He helped me put the roof on the house before winter set in. Bud Lofstedt took me out again in August to get my meat for winter. We heard that the caribou were migrating through Eureka, and it was the November hunting season. Vince had a 1959 Rambler station wagon that worked great for hunting. The seats would fold down to sleep, and there was room to haul game and a place for the antlers on the roof rack. We loaded up our gear Monday and took off for Eureka. Sometimes KFQD radio in Anchorage would announce when and where to find the caribou. It could be both good and bad because the soldiers from Fort Richardson Army Base would show up in great numbers.

Vince and I stopped at Eureka Lodge for a bite to eat and to hear all the hunting news. We then drove past Eureka and back to a gravel pit to park for the night. We talked awhile and then slipped off our rubber insulated boots and climbed into our sleeping bags. We knew it was going to be cold that night but down to -40 degrees to -45 degrees was ridiculous. By morning the frost from our breathing had coated the windows about 1/8-inch thick. Vince only had to slide his seat and start the engine. We stayed in our bags till the car warmed up. I got out of my bag and went to put on my boots. But my right one was frozen like a rock in a crimped position. I was able to get the left boot on and finally with difficulty got the right boot on my foot. It was difficult jumping on one foot until the other foot warmed up the boot.

We decided to have some breakfast, but at that temperature and at six it was not too appealing. Vince tried to thaw out a can of fruit cocktail, and to do so he fixed up a propane torch. It scorched the fruit on the bottom by the time the top thawed enough to get a spoon into it. Well, so much for breakfast. We decided we would wait until it was daylight to start out. So back in the car we went. It was finally light enough to see, so we took the white aukeo off the top of the carrier and tied on our pack .The aukeo was an army surplus toboggan made of fiberglass used to haul wounded soldiers.

We came to the end of the gravel pit and saw where the road went down into the valley. It was steep and there was probably two feet of snow on the ground. We went down the road, Vince in the lead and me with the anchor rope on the rear of the aukeo to keep it from running over Vince. We went across the valley and up the other side walking along the ridge. We heard a vehicle coming up the hill behind us. Looking down in the valley, we saw seven caribou trotting along, going the same direction we were traveling. We didn't let on about the caribou. The pickup with its wheels spinning and two soldiers behind pushing with all their might passed us. About fifteen minutes after they had passed, we heard shooting up ahead; looking up the valley, we saw the caribou coming our way. Vince started down over the hill to head them off. An open area lay about halfway down the hill. So I decided to ride the aukeo. I was picking up speed, and I was running out of open hill.

There were alder bushes ahead, and fortunately they grow out and downhill so the stalks pointed away from me, and I rode up the branches, flying ten to fifteen feet in the air. I landed at the bottom of the hill about the same time as Vince. He had already started to shoot from the edge of the hill. I grabbed my gun and took aim and shot. We both got our limit of two caribou. We praised the Lord for answered prayer. With four caribou, it would take us more than one trip. We cut up two caribou and loaded what we could. We then decided to do the other two because of the cold. They could freeze pretty stiff, making it harder to skin and cut up. We started through the valley toward the road when we saw the 2x2 pickup on the road and three soldiers standing at the tailgate talking and laughing. We were wondering what a 2x2 pickup was doing down in the valley. As we walked up and inquired, one GI said, "Oh, I yelled at George here to stop, but he just kept right on going and here we are." They had to hire an army surplus weasel track vehicle from Eureka Lodge to pull them out and to the gravel pit.

Less than twenty-four hours since our arrival, we had our caribou and were ready to head home. No more overnight camping for us at this temperature.

CHAPTER 9

Backyard Encounter

Each winter at Solid Rock Bible Camp, I would try to get a log cabin built for boys. I was working on Cabin # 3 and putting a log in place. This process began by pouring the concrete piers in late fall before freeze-up so the cabin could be built through the winter. My equipment was a chainsaw, axe wedges, an old green Dodge pickup given to the camp, a long rope, and two pulleys. I would cut down selected spruce from what later became the ski hill. I would cut them into lengths, skid them down to the camp road, and then, by a pulley on a tree, skid them from the road to the cabin site on the hill. I would peel the logs with a spudder made from a crosscut saw blade created by Nick Leman. The log would be laid on the wall with a small block on one end and the chainsaw blade run between the logs to flatten both sides. Reverse the block and go through again. Fiberglass insulation was then stapled to the bottom log. Corners were notched and fitted, then drilled and spiked down.

I was about halfway up on the wall when my wife screamed that there was a bear up at the house, and Scott, seven years old, was playing in the yard. I jumped in the pickup, my 30- 06, on the gun rack, and I drove up the hill to our house driveway. Scott by then was standing at the bottom of the tree, looking up in wonder at the black bear hanging on the tree. I took Scott over to the house and handed him to his mother. The bear was still up the tree, so I shot it. One dead bear landed at my feet. I dressed him out and hung him for a few days. Butchered him for the freezer and winter eating.

CHAPTER 10

Blowing My Own Horn

A young gal had received Christ as Savior during evangelistic meetings at Kenai Bible Church. Mac McElveen was the preacher. Marge was concerned for her brother Bill, age twenty-three, who claimed to be an agnostic. He was coming to Alaska to hunt, and she asked Mac if he would take him hunting and trusted he would come to Christ during the hunting trip. Brother Mac called me and asked if I would go along. I had room for caribou in my freezer and the challenge to share Christ was exciting, so I agreed.

We picked up Bill in Kenai and drove my 1960 Rambler station wagon with our gear to the Lake Louise area about fifty miles short of Glennallen and about a hundred miles closer than our last hunt on the Denali Hwy. We had heard on the radio that there were caribou there. We turned at the highway and drove down the winding road toward Lake Louise while telling stories of hunting adventures. It was cold and dark with hard-packed snow on the road. We stopped at the Lake Louise Lodge and decided to go inside and have coffee, and maybe find out the location of the caribou. The owner had two dogs and a mynah bird, and when we went in they started barking. We saw the two dogs that barked but couldn't figure out from where the third dog was barking. To our surprise it was the mynah bird that barked like a dog. We laughed and chatted and drank more coffee, trying to stay up as late as possible and enjoy the warm lodge.

About eleven the owner wanted to close up, and so I asked him if we could sleep out front in our station wagon. He consented, realizing we couldn't afford rooms. We went out and put the seats down, Bill on the far right, Mac in the middle, and I was behind the steering wheel. We got to sleep.

Suddenly at two in the morning, the car horn began to blow, and the dogs and the mynah bird were barking as I struggled to get my foot out of the horn ring. We all sat up with a jolt, laughing but wondering if the owner would be out with a gun to drive us off.

The clouds rolled away and the moon came out full, and it was really light on the snow. We couldn't see the moon from our position, so we thought it was getting daylight. We decided to get out and prepare breakfast on the tailgate. We had a can of peaches, and I don't remember what else. We decided to get back in the car and wait till it was light enough to hunt. I turned on the radio, and we found out it was three-thirty in the morning.

The Lord knew how our day was going to go with little time to talk to Bill, so He got us awake in an unusual way. Mac told us later he felt it was now or never, and the Lord was leading him to share the gospel. Mac began by asking Bill how he would like to be lost in the deep woods of Alaska in this cold wasteland, and Bill didn't like the thought of it. We talked about people who had been lost and some who didn't get out alive; those who did were terrified of the experience. Then Mac said to Bill, "What if you were lost in this vast wilderness and didn't know how to get out, but along came a man who offered you a map showing you exactly how to get out to civilization. Would you accept it?"

Bill said he would. Then Mac went on to explain how God has given us His road map so that we can find our way out of this wilderness of far worse consequences than anything in life. Mac took his New Testament and opened the Word of God and presented salvation through the Lord Jesus Christ. Mac and I took turns sharing, and I gave my testimony. One would talk, the other pray and vice versa. Mac said, "Bill, will you accept

Jesus Christ as your personal Lord and Savior?" He said yes, and we prayed, and he prayed to receive Christ. We were praising the Lord. I said, "This is wonderful. Our main purpose has been answered, so I know God is going to give us our caribou."

We had a hill to go up, and it was slippery. We tried several times; finally Mac and Bill got out pushed and prayed it over the top. We waited till it got light enough to see and shoot. We prayed and thanked God for the caribou we believed He was going to provide. We started driving back out Lake Louise road from the lodge, and within just a few miles caribou crossed in front of us. We shot our caribou, cleaned and skinned them, and headed home before noon.

We look back and see how God's plan was fulfilled in the timing: the moon, getting my foot stuck in the horn, Bill's prepared heart, and time to talk to him. It was a fabulous, trip but far better than the hunt for caribou was Bill's finding Christ as his Savior. The caribou sustained our physical life for a time, but Bill will be with us in heaven forever.

Successful caribou hunt for Bert and Mac.

CHAPTER 11

Homesteading

Alaskan pioneers, like all pioneers even from the early days of settling the West, are a special breed: adventurous, hardworking, independent, and often stubborn. They had to build roads and clear a percentage of the land on their homestead. One hundred sixty down to forty acres were available for homesteading: building a house or cabin and living on the land for a year. A crop had to be planted and was inspected by the government agent. This was called *proving up*, in order to get their title deed. It was a backbreaking, difficult process and hard on the family.

The 1948 Kenai forest fire provided charred kiln-dried spruce for their stoves' fuel and logs for their homes. There were few jobs in the area, so many men worked in Anchorage for the winter. Their families were alone and faced many hardships. Some women were the breadwinners in the family and found work away from home as nurses or teachers. Men and women developed the homesteads. Many had to abandon their dream because of sickness or unemployment, or couldn't prove up on the land and had to relinquish it to another.

Homesteading began after the Second World War, and many GIs became homesteaders. Those who proved up, homesteading along the Sterling Highway, did well in being able to sell property after oil was discovered in the Swanson River area.

The Northland Baptist Church was granted land in Sterling, Alaska, in the middle of homesteading country. President Dwight Eisenhower signed the title.

CHAPTER 12

Lost and Found Fishing Rod

Brother Mac, living in Cooper Landing, knew the fishing streams well. We both fished the Russian River, and there would be no one around, even in the peak of the salmon run. Donna's folks came to visit from Pennsylvania in 1959, and Dad Porte loved to fish. Mac invited us to come up to Cooper Landing to go fishing on the Russian River.

King salmon and a lot of red salmon spawn up the Russian River and into Lower and Upper Russian Lakes. We fished well below the falls on the Russian River and had a blast. Mac and I were catching those beautiful eight-to-ten pound reds. Dad kept losing his line, hooks, and weight, so he found a piece of heavy line and tied it to the last loop on his rod. He said he was going to catch one and *horse* it in without breaking the heavy line.

After a few casts, he snagged a king salmon and it started upstream. He couldn't hold the rod up or hold the fish back, so he let the fish run and forward went the rod. It pulled in two at the junction, and away went the top half of his rod. He was heartsick to lose part of his new rod. Mac and I walked over to where he was fishing, and Dad explained what happened. We prayed for the Lord to somehow help us get the rod back. As we were standing there, we saw the top of the rod swirl around in the pool in front of us. Mac cast his line and hook at it a couple times. Finally his hook caught in one of the eyes of the rod end. The king took off upstream; Mac held on and fought till the fish tore off the hook, and he reeled in Dad's fishing pole.

After thinking things over, we realized that the king had a spawning partner in that pool and had come back to the place Dad had snagged him. Dad Porte was happy to get his rod back and get his limit of fish.

Meeting of the bulls.

Twin moose calves.

Scott combat fishing on the Kenai River

Solid Rock Horse Pack Trip

CHAPTER 13

Caribou on Fourth Avenue

Brother Mac, his wife Virginia, and family were asked by their mission agency to start a new work in Anchorage. So the Van Sickles took over at Cooper Landing, and my hunting buddy Mac was gone. Frank Rusk was on the camp executive board. He had a sawmill on his homestead at Clam Gulch, and we sawed logs for the camp craft shop and a couple cabins.

Frank had a big furniture van that he wanted to take on a caribou hunting trip and invited me to go along. Harley Fellers, and old-timer from Kasilof, joined us. Harley had helped me peel logs at camp, and everyone called him Uncle Harley. Frank believed in all the comforts of home, and he took a full size bed, Coleman stove, and all the equipment necessary. I offered him a canvas cot that had heavy metal legs that slipped into sockets, and he just laughed. Well, the laugh was on me because I took one for

Uncle Harley and ended up one leg short for the two cots. I had to prop the foot end up with my duffle bag.

We headed up the highway for Lake Louise and got there in the early afternoon. There was a snow cover of four to six inches on the ground. This made it good to spot caribou on the ridges. With three of us in the cab, it was a bit crowded, and I suggested I ride up on top of the van above the passenger side to spot caribou. The signal was to kick the side of the van if I saw caribou, and Frank would stop. We were going down a medium-grade hill when I saw three caribou off to the left coming toward the road. I began to kick on the van side, and Frank saw the caribou approaching the road. So he sped up going down the hill to get close enough for a shot as they were breaking across in front of us. Then Frank hit the brakes and I came off the roof, my feet hit the hood, and the next giant step landed me on the road. He literally flung me off the top of the truck. I was scrambling to stay up with my body ahead of my legs. My gun, slung over my shoulder, clobbered me on the back of the head. How I stayed on my feet, only the Lord knows. By then the caribou were running fast across the muskeg. I cranked a shell into the chamber as I came to a halt, wheezing, panting, and trying to hold my breath for a shot. When I shot, the fuzz flew off the tail of the caribou like a child would blow a dandelion gone to seed. That quick, the caribou had reached the brush and disappeared.

That night we pulled into a gravel pit, fixed a good supper, pulled the rear doors shut, and went to bed. It was cold that night, and the cold came up through the canvas cot and through my sleeping bag. Next morning Frank said, "Now you know why I brought my bed." Uncle Harley didn't do much better, but he had a heavier sleeping bag. We had a good breakfast and asked the Lord to provide us with caribou that day so we could head home and get out of the cold.

We decided to check out the woods below the gravel pit. There were fresh tracks all over, so we knew caribou were around. About then we heard shots to the left, and as we watched, we saw caribou moving through the trees in single file on a hillside trail. A big bull was leading the group, and they were moving parallel to us at about seventy-five yards. The lead bull stopped for a moment, confused by those other hunters and possibly smelling us. I sat down and told Harley, "I think I can get that bull from here." I pulled up and shot for his shoulder, and he went up on his hind legs like a horse and disappeared.

We discovered that the shots we heard were from a group of GIs from the military base. They spooked the caribou herd, and they were running all around us in the trees. It seemed like a war broke out as shots were being fired. We were shooting caribou, and so were the GIs who didn't know we were there. When a bullet whistled by my head, I grabbed Uncle Harley, and we jumped in a depression among the hummocks. I took my camp whistle and blew if for all I was worth. I yelled, "Somebody's going to get killed."

The shooting stopped, and the hunters whom we had never seen disappeared. They must have thought I said somebody is killed because they forgot about caribou and even the ones they shot.

We decided to stop shooting also and count the total of dead caribou. I went to check on the big bull, and from where I hit him, he staggered another forty feet into some brush and died. We counted up the caribou, and we had eleven. In those days you were allowed four per hunter. We were allowed to shoot one more, but decided to call it enough. We dragged them all to a mossy bank near the gravel pit, gutted and quartered them, but left the hides on to keep them clean. What a pile of meat! It was good we had a truck and not a station wagon or we would have been in big trouble. Frank cooked up some grub while Harley and I finished the last caribou.

It was getting dark, and Frank didn't want to start out on the long drive, so we decided to spend another night. Frank enjoyed the comfort of his bed. We got awake early, had breakfast, and set off toward Anchorage. Can you imagine loading forty-four quarters of caribou in the back of the truck and taking off down the road?

We were around Eagle River when Frank asked how much caribou Harley and I wanted. I said the big bull would be all I could handle with a moose and fish already in my freezer. Uncle Harley said he only had room for one small caribou, so Frank was left to handle the rest. He informed us that his freezer broke down, and he had to stop in Anchorage to buy a large new chest freezer. The worst was yet to come.

We drove down Fourth Avenue to the Northern Commercial Company and pulled up to the curb. Frank told us to unload the caribou on the curb so we could get the freezer in the front of the truck. Harley slid the caribou on the tailgate, and I set it in rows along the curb. It was a sight to behold. Within five minutes we had a crowd of a dozen people stopping and asking where we got all the caribou. We just told them Lake Louise Road. We were eating a piece of cake when Frank came out and told us the bad news: no freezer in the store but they had one at the warehouse. So we loaded up the caribou, and the curious left when we pulled away.

We backed up to the loading dock at the Northern Commercial and unloaded the caribou onto the platform, which was a little easier than the curb. We should have waited to unload. The freezer that the store said they had was gone. But they said we could have the display model at the Fourth Avenue store. After reloading the caribou, off we went to the Fourth Avenue store. This time we made sure we could get the demonstrator; then we unloaded the caribou again onto the sidewalk. By now many people were coming home from work, and this unusual sight of caribou meat stacked along the sidewalk drew a bigger crowd with many questions of where we got the caribou. The store crew and Frank came out with the freezer and lifted it up into the bed of the van. We pushed it into place and hoped we loaded the caribou for the last time.

That episode today would have made the news and also alerted the police. We laughed about that incident for years, but it wasn't funny then. Need I say we sure enjoyed that caribou meat, and it seemed very tender. I wonder why?

CHAPTER 14

The Earthquake

On March 27, 1964, I was cutting the roof rafter pattern for the new craft shop at Solid Rock Bible Camp. A friend stopped by from the Kasilof Children's Home to see how the work was progressing. He said before he left, "Bert, did you ever cut your SKILSAW cord in half?"

My reply was, "No, I never did a dumb thing like that."

After he left, I picked up the saw, ready to cut the pencil mark on the rafter, when the cord got caught in the guard and my cord went in two with sparks flying. I began to wonder why that happened, for either he was possessed or I was being humbled.

I was sitting on the sawhorse, splicing the saw cord and beginning to tape it, when things began to move. At first I thought I was dizzy, but quickly I knew it was an earthquake. However, this one kept getting stronger and stronger. I swung my leg over the sawhorse, and before I knew it,I was riding a bucking sawhorse and holding on with both hands. It's impossible to believe everything around you and under you can move that much. It was noisy too, as Miracle Lake ice broke up about fifteen feet from shore, forming a black silt circle. The Memorial Lodge was swaying side to side. The chimney that rose from the fireplace beneath, through the second story, and above the peak came crashing down. The cement blocks spewed out the mortar between them.

I looked back toward the Rock and Miracle Lake to the parked 1960 International bus. It was swaying back and forth. The front rims were up on blocks. The wheels had been removed to use on a logging truck. Ula Smith and Marie Barber's new camping trailer was parked next to the bus. Barb was Solid Rock's Craft Director, and Ula was a Bible teacher. I thought the bus was about to fall right on the little camper, and I prayed out loud, "Oh, Lord, please save the camper." The Lord answered. The blocks fell out and the bus settled down. Finally after four and a half minutes, the 9.5 quake was over.

But before it stopped, I yelled for Donna to see if she was all right, and she answered me. I ran up the hill, staggering to the house about a hundred yards away. Donna and Scott, eight years old, had trouble getting out of the moving doorway of the house. Unable to stand, they were sitting in the driveway. They were afraid the swaying trees would snap off and had tried to get in our car, but it was bouncing like a rubber ball.

The next day I went down to survey the damage. My tracks in the snow looked like the steps of a drunk. The dishes in the lodge had flown off the shelves and were broken. The wagon wheel lights swung so badly, they broke the chimney shades and bulbs.

The fireplace hearth was bare except for the Heatilator. The blocks were stacked up against the back of the piano and strewn out to the middle support pole. The kitchen was a wreck. The damage was about twelve hundred dollars, which is what it cost to get camp back into shape for the coming summer. Frank Rusk and I rebuilt the fireplace with stone.

CHAPTER 15

Swamp Trail

In the late sixties, Bob Schmidt introduced me to the Fuller Lake trail country and beyond. They were horseback trips that made packing moose a lot easier. Bob had a huge gelding named Blondie that he always rode, and I rode Lady. We took Flata as a packhorse because that is all she ever knew. An old sourdough trapper and miner owned her, and he never rode her, especially since he didn't want thrown off.

We hauled the horses with a four-place trailer to the trail head parking lot, which was a gravel pit next to the Sterling Highway. We loaded Flata with our gear and food, and all we had to carry was a sleeping bag tied behind the saddle and our gun slung over our shoulder. It's about four miles in to the one end of the lake and about six miles before you get to the other end where the lake creek flows out. There's a nice place to camp and a good place to spot the high grassy meadows scattered around and between the alder patches.

Usually, the next morning we could spot moose in the openings or along the edge nibbling on alder or willow. We would ride in that direction and get as close as we could before going on foot. Back in those days the moose didn't seem to be bothered by horses because they were just another big animal like them. And maybe the horse smell drowned out the smell of humans.

The previous year we both got our bulls in this vicinity. We kept this base camp for the whole hunt, which lasted about four days. As always, I prayed for the Lord to provide my moose and He did.

Bob had been coming in here to hunt several years before with his brother, Rodger, so things were beginning to change. In fact, there were horse hoof prints we had seen earlier, and now at our old camping spot, we came up empty after a day and a half. Bob had explored previously a new area that no one had gone into, at least not from this direction. It was called Dyke Creek Valley. There was only one way from this direction to get through over the saddle and down into the valley. You had to go through brush, some alder, and worst of all a swamp that had a muddy bottom. Bob found this out in his exploration the year before when Blondie almost got stuck. Bob hooked onto her with the pack horse and pulled her out. After much searching, he found one place you could go through, but one has to hit it right on the money. Fifteen feet to either side, you would be in trouble.

Bob was doing some thinking about Dyke Creek because we were only seeing a few cows and no bulls. The morning of the third day, he decided to try to ford our way through the bog and down into Dyke Creek Valley. We packed up our camp after breakfast and headed out east from camp back across the Fuller Lake Creek. There was a good two miles of trail to where it came to an abrupt stop. From there it was pick our way through trees and brush, and skirt the alder patches.

Bob would stop and look, and then go back and turn left, trying to find the exact spot. Blondie and my horse were both wondering what he was doing, and Flata, being led by Bob, was one confused packhorse. Finally, after almost getting Flata stuck, Bob managed to pull her back out of the swamp and find the one area we could go through. We crossed the divide up ahead and down over the other side to Dyke Creek.

What a beautiful spot. From where we set up camp, you could look up to a high ridge that circled all the around in front of us, like the half of a football stadium. Only this stadium had beautiful green bushes and meadows scattered all the way around, tier after tier, till they reached the altitude where trees didn't grow and the bushes stopped to give way to the rocks and high country.

We got off of our horses and glassed the hills. There was a bull moose to the right and one directly to my left about halfway up the rise. Both were feeding along the alder bushes, and you could see the bushes move when they stripped off the leaves as they fed. It was early afternoon with time to get them back to camp before dark, if everything went right.

We dropped the gear and tied the horses, and both of us started in different directions, picking our way on side hill moose trails to get as close as we could. Bob got to his first because I heard the shot, then a pause and another—that I figured was the final shot, and it was.

I came around the downside of the alder patch, unsure where my moose was located. I went cautiously on foot. After searching the field, I realized it must be the next patch over and ahead. I moved on slowly and stepped out the bottom side of the field where alder and grass met and listened. I heard him moving the alder and eating, so I slowly moved in his direction, crouching in the high grass. I finally saw him at about fifty yards. He still didn't know I was around. I took off my safety, and since he was standing almost broadside except for his head and neck, I placed the shot in his hump. Thump, down he went, and I knew he wasn't going anywhere. He was another nice three to four years old with a rack spread in the low forties. I praised the Lord and let out a yell, and Bob answered. We both worked on our own moose to get them ready for the packhorse. Bob brought two quarters down to camp on Blondie and then came to help me. We got all the meat out and hung up at camp for the night.

The next morning we had breakfast while watching seven rams (Dahl sheep) on the rocks beyond where the amphitheater turned and came around to our far right. With the scope, you could see five were full curl, one was a curl and a quarter, and the other was about three-quarter curl. Wow! What a sight to make your blood boil. I had never shot a ram. Bob agreed to let me go after one.

This area was beyond the closed area for hunting sheep. I climbed up behind the rocks and up over the top, which took me a good hour. I knew the big ram was by himself over the rise below me. I made my way slowly up to the top, but there were always more large rocks and mountain jags sticking up, and I couldn't see over. Finally, I got where I could see over, but the ram moved to the left behind some more rocks. And just as I was creeping around that rock that blocked my view, a rock squirrel or marmot was sitting there watching, and he left out a chirp, to warn the ram. He was already heading away and down the mountain. It happened so fast, I didn't even get a shot off.

When I got back to camp, Bob was giving me the raspberries and finally said, "It is good you didn't get him; we have enough to pack out."

We were all day making two trips, leading three horses down to the highway.

You were wondering about the swamp? Going the other way and backtracking, the trail came right to the spot where we could cross in a few inches of water and a solid bottom.

CHAPTER 16

A Tumbling Horse

Bob Schmidt had given the camp four of his horses, so we were able to start a horse program at Solid Rock Bible Camp. We used to go on our moose hunt using Bob's horse trailer. I just had to introduce my son, Scott, to the beautiful Fuller Lake region, which I was very familiar with by now. We made it without problem to the gravel pit parking area and unloaded the horses, tied our pack behind our saddles, and began our adventure.

Again, I was overwhelmed as we climbed the trail on that beautiful August day. You could look back and see the lake-filled valley and the mountains crystal clear in the early afternoon. We made our way around the first small lake and meandered between it and big Fuller Lake. The trail rose about 150 to 200 feet along the mountain to the right of the lake with the billowing clouds reflected in the lake that was like a mirror. The trail descended back down and crossed the stream that brought us to our first camp site. Much to our amazement, as we glassed to our left, a steep side hill lay to the left about seventy-five yards away, and a moose slowly made his way up the mountain. I pointed and motioned for Scott to get off his horse and come to me. I held both horses' reins as he took the gun and scoped in on the moose, which stopped and looked back. Scott shot, and the moose fell behind some rocks. We tied the horses to some alder and scurried up the mountain as fast as we could. Talk about excitement and being out of breath. We had to approach carefully because I mentioned almost getting kicked before by a down but live moose. Sure enough, he was still alive but couldn't get up, so Scott shot him behind the ear, and it was all over.

It was difficult working on that moose on that steep hillside, but the worst was yet to come. We got the moose quartered and ready to pack out. We descended the mossy hill, sliding partway back to our horses. We brought Flata up first because she was a good packer. We had the moose quarters in game bags, hoisted them up one at a time, and tied one on each side with the leg bones together tied to the saddle horn and the stirrups tied up as a cradle for the shanks. It was difficult for the horse to stand on that steep side hill, and she got more and more nervous. Just as I was about to lead her down, the saddle slid to the downhill side, swinging both meat quarters, and toppled the horse over and down the mountain. She rolled for about twenty-five feet and came to a stop in the low bushes. I ran down the hill to try to untie anything, but before I got to her, she staggered to her feet enough to topple over and roll on down the mountain. Once her behind went right over her head, and I was praying she wouldn't break her neck. She stopped on a large pile of brush, and this time I got to her before she could get up.

She didn't want to move. The problem became clear. When we tightened the belly band, she breathed out so it wouldn't be so tight. So we needed to knee her a bit in the side so she would breathe in when we cinched the strap. Also, after you ride that far, you need to tighten the cinch, especially before you load game meat on the saddle. It was my fault for not catching that problem. I untied everything so she could get back on her feet. This time the saddle was tightened real tight, and we put the meat back on and made it down to the trail and back to where we were going to camp. The second trip was without incident, and we got all the meat back to camp and hung up for the night to come. From where we were camped, it was about five miles back to the highway and the trailer.

The next day, after a good breakfast, we decided to head home; leading a horse down is much easier than packing that moose on your back. If I remember right, we got a good three hundred pounds of meat boned out and packaged for winter, and Scott was thrilled to get his first moose at age fifteen.

CHAPTER 17

Fuller Lake Hunting Trip

I hadn't hunted with Bob Schmidt for a few years, so I called him to see if he would take his horses for a trip up to Fuller Lake and beyond. It was after fishing had closed on Cook Inlet, and he was tired and needed a break. We loaded up Blondie and Lady into the horse trailer and headed for the Cooper Landing area. This time we didn't take a packhorse. We decided we would both walk and lead our own horse with the meat packs.

We parked in the gravel pit, locked the pickup, prepared our packs and gear, and started up the trail with Bob in the lead. The trees were turning color, the sky was blue with billowy clouds, and the trail was in normal condition with wet spots. The higher we climbed, the more beautiful the scene became. We saw the lake-filled valley and snow-capped mountains in the distance. We went around Fuller Lake where water ran down through the grass from the hillsides. By then we meandered through grass and past clumps of small birch and aspen. Along the upper part of the lake, it is wide open with the mountains going up on each side of Upper Fuller Lake. The trail around the far side winds up a hundred feet. We looked down at the crystal clear water with the clouds reflecting the beauty of the sky. Black bears had been spotted eating berries up on the hillside between the alder patches.

The trail descends back down to the lake. At the lake's end, the trail goes across a rocky area with boulders marking the spot of the creek that drains from the lake. Just beyond is a flat area above the creek that was a camping spot for many years and where I had camped at least twice before and in the future would camp with my sons.

We glassed the same areas, as we did on the other trips, and saw only cow moose grazing in the open areas on the far hill between the alders. We had some supper and relaxed, talking about other hunting experiences. That night I was reading from Philippians 4 KJV for my quiet time, and Bob wanted to listen. I came to Philippians 4:19 and read, "My God shall supply all your needs according to His riches in Glory." Bob had been a bit down spiritually, and I wanted this trip to be a time to draw closer to the Lord in our Christian faith.

I said, "Bob, there is the promise we need, and I am going to take it as God's promise to us for this hunt. I believe with all my heart He is going to provide each of us with a moose." He thought it was good, but I'm not sure at this point how strongly he believed because as yet we hadn't seen a bull.

The next morning after breakfast we decided, after glassing the hills to no avail, to go on ahead to the next overlook, which allowed us to see out over the Sterling Flats with a nice valley coming out to the left. We got moose here in previous years, but after glassing most of the morning, we saw nothing but cows. Over in the valley about two miles away, we could see a couple of bulls that had some cows with them, and they were going farther away. It was a swampy area, and no horse trail led down into that mucky area. We went back to our old camp, took a left at the fork of another trail, and rode for about a half hour.

The first valley to the right had a trail through the bottom, and the next valley over was Dyke Creek. Bob stayed in the valley and I rode on a moose trail up the hillside and began to glass the area. Bob went over along the opposite hill and disappeared in the trees. There was a clearing between us, and as I was watching, I saw movement in the clearing. It was so far off, I had to look close to see what it was. It was a moose walking straight in my direction. As the moose walked, it would turn and look back to its left.

I realized later that he heard Bob in the brush and was moving out. The sun through the trees would glint on his head and reveal what looked to me like small horns. You have to be careful because a moose has big ears, and small horns can be hard to distinguish. As the moose made a right turn across the field, it looked now like two ears on the left side of his head, and the sun reflected a glint of shine. I looked through my scope. I could barely make out the small palm with about two points. He stopped for a moment to listen, and it was then I prayed. "Lord, please give me that moose." It would take a miracle because he was only 1/4-to-3/8 inches in length through the scope. Bob figured later that I was 150 to 175 yards away. I held my breath and held high over his back, and I was shooting downhill. The first shot rang out, and the moose shuddered but didn't go down. I missed with the second shot, and on the third shot he went down, an incredible kill. Bob came out of the woods on his horse, looked up at me, and scratched his head. He thought someone else was hunting in the area. I yelled that I shot a moose, pointed, and waved him in the direction of the moose.

I got on Lady and rode down the steep hill into the field where Bob was standing. I said, "Is it a bull?"

Still not positive, and Bob said, "You ought to be ashamed shooting such a little suckling."

"What! Is it a bull?" I said as I looked, and Bob said, "Yes, it's a bull," much to my relief. He was big enough for my family of four.

After we gutted him, it was time to get a moose for Bob. God had provided for me, and I was sure God had a moose for Bob. We left the small bull and prayed the Lord would keep the bears away until we packed him out. We headed on up the valley, and near the other end was a huge rock outcropping where the trail went around each side. It stood by itself on the side of the valley. We decided to split up; I took the trail to the left up along the hillside, and Bob went to the right on the other side of the outcropping.

My trail went up the side hill and circled around between two big alder bushes. Just as I approached the bushes, my horse flinched and jumped to the side. A big bull was coming around toward me around the bush to my right. He tore into the center of the alder patch and disappeared. I yelled for Bob. "I have your moose cornered." He heard me yell and came riding up on Blondie from behind me. I explained what happened and showed him where the bull disappeared into the alder patch. He told me to go around to the right and watch, which I did.

Bob rode Blondie into the opening in the alder patch, but the horse would not go through. She went up on hind legs and let a few neighs in revolt. Bob tried to make her go, but she wouldn't. I heard the fracas, and then everything was quiet. I started to ride on ahead around the patch when I heard a shot, then a second. Bob backed out of the patch and rode around the left side and saw the moose taking off. He jumped off his horse and shot the bull behind the ear. It fell beside a bubbling creek coming down the hill. I said, "Praise the Lord. He is faithful. I told you God would come through on His promise."

And Bob smiled and said, "This is amazing."

What a place to butcher a moose. We cleaned it, cleaned our tools and ourselves, packed the moose on our horses, and walked back to the other moose. We had too much for the horses, so we had to make two trips out to the truck and trailer in order to get both moose packed out. Bob's moose was about a five year old with a fifty-three-inch rack. Mine was measurable, but you can't eat the horns anyway. That trip accomplished my goal of seeing both of us encouraged in the Lord.

CHAPTER 18

Moose Twins

In my ministry at Solid Rock Bible Camp, we didn't have a winter program except at Christmas vacation time. So besides my building, and Donna and I planning for the summer, I would pastor a mission church for six months. The missionary usually went *outside* (the lower forty-eight states) to do deputation speaking in supporting churches. I was pastor of Kenai Bible Church on two occasions and twice pastor of the Kasilof Community Church for Ray Mainwaring. I also preached on Sundays for a summer at Ninilchik.

I was at Kasilof doing visitation from house to house, cabin to cabin, sharing Christ and praying with the people. It was fall and pouring rain. I needed a moose, and the season was starting. I had no hunting trip planned, no one to go with, and I didn't know where to go. A day or two before, I had asked a friend about a good place to hunt. His instructions were to go back to the pipeline road, before the mountain at the end of the flats, and the gate would be open for hunters. I was to drive back to the pipeline and turn right and cross over a questionable stream. The stream had a hard bottom and with a 4x4 vehicle was passable. Reaching the top of the hill, I was told to look off to the left and I would see moose. I almost chuckled to think it would be that easy. I prayed for direction about the trip. When I got back home, the weather was good toward the mountains, and I took it as a sign that He had a moose for me.

I packed my gear, gun, food, pack board, and butchering tools, and set out with the camp's old 4x4 Dodge Power Wagon. I followed Jack's directions to a tee. I turned right on the gas line road and came to the creek. Then there was an old wooden footbridge that was about rotted out. I put the rig in four low and drove right through the rushing stream. I drove up the two-track pipeline access road and stopped at the top of the hill and looked off to my left. There to my amazement were two bull moose; both had thirty-six to forty-inch racks, and both were busy munching the willow as if they were starved. They must have been twins because they were exactly the same size and same racks. I was only fifty yards from them. They didn't run or pay any attention to me. They were facing me with bush between us.

I got out of the 4x4 very quietly and rested my gun on a leaning tree. I put the crosshair on the high chest of the one on the left and fired. He disappeared from sight, and the next thing I knew he was running across an open area and along the side hill, now at seventy-five yards. So I pulled up and shot him on the run, and down he went. I ran over to where he was lying, and he was trying to get up. I had shot him in his back leg, and he couldn't get up. I thought, "Oh no, I shot him in the neck with a good steady scope; there is something wrong." I went across to the other spot, and there lay my first moose.

I was sick at heart and didn't know what to do. I gutted the first bull, and propped open his ribs. The other moose was still down but would get nervous when I approached and would try to get up.

Just then my prayer was answered. A pickup camper drove in the road on the other side of the creek, turned around, and stopped. I ran over to the 4x4 and turned the key. The starter turned over, but the Dodge would not start. I tried two or three times, and the battery began to get weak. I prayed, "Please, Lord, start this thing so I can get help." The next try it barely caught and fired up. I was so thankful and drove over to the camper. I got out and knocked on the camper door. A man came and opened the door with a pistol in his hands. I said, "I suppose you are here to hunt moose."

And he said, "Yeah."

I told him, "I already have a moose for you, but you will have to kill it." Then I explained.

We went back over in my rig and went to where the moose was lying. It was twilight and the light was poor. We looked around for what seemed to be fifteen minutes, and finally I said, "Let's just stand still and listen carefully. He is wounded and will surely stir and make noise." We waited for several minutes. There was a noise in the grass about twenty-five feet from us. The GI shot the moose in the heart, and it was all over.

Now comes the fun and work of dressing out the moose. With two people, it is a lot easier. I remember times dressing out a moose myself, and you are straddling the carcass, cutting him down the chest and belly, when his hind legs shoots by and whacks you in the side of the head. That hoof is much harder than my head.

We propped open the GI's moose to cool and decided to go to bed and meet early in the morning to get the moose. I got back to my rig full of thanks for the way it worked out.

We had a good half-day's work between us, and we worked well together. I had prayed for opportunity to share Jesus with him. I asked him if he went to church, and he said, "My wife goes, but one evening the preacher came to my house and wanted me to pay my tithe to the church. That's all he wanted was money."

I told him that God didn't want his money and explained what a Christian was and how to become one. I explained that God wants him to be His child and explained the plan of salvation. There were times when he resisted, so I would drop it and we would talk about other things and then come back again to the Lord. He never warmed up to his need of Christ, so all I could do was pray for him.

We packed out the moose and put it in our rigs. His wife took a picture of us in front of the truck with our racks and our guns. I thanked him, and he thanked me, and I thanked God.

.

CHAPTER 19

Returning the Favor

When my dad and mom, Otto and Edna Schultz, at sixty-six years of age, came to Alaska, it was an exciting time. Donna and I wanted them to see the growing ministry at Solid Rock Bible Camp and to experience the great land. This is the first time they had ever flown in an airplane, so it was a big decision to come all the way from Pittsburgh.

Dad used to take me fishing for trout in Spruce Creek, Pennsylvania, and we hunted for rabbits, so I was going to have the time of my life being the guide for him on this trip. There is a chain of lakes on the Swan Lake Canoe Trails. A friend of mine told me about a group of three lakes that feed each other about half mile to the left of the east gate of the trails. The identification mark was a large rock next to the road just past the trail entrance.

Dad and I found it without any trouble. He took our food pack and bags for the fish. I packed the seventeen-foot fiberglass canoe on my shoulders with a life jacket for padding. A built-in seat shoulder rest just wide enough for packing helped. The only problem was that the distance was not a half mile but about three- quarters of a mile, and the canoe weighed seventy five pounds. The trail only went a short distance, and then it was pick and choose between small birch trees that were fairly close together. The turning and twisting through the woods was tiresome and downright exhausting till we finally sighted the lake through the trees. Within minutes we were launched with our gear and paddles. Our fishing gear was simple enough with a light fly rod, a ball of lead the size of a green pea, a single hook, and single salmon egg.

It was a gorgeous day with billowing clouds above and the sun peeking in and out between the clouds. As soon as you would cast in the green lily pads, the lead and egg hit the bottom, and bang, you had a Dolly Varden or a rainbow on the line. The fish were all twelve to fifteen inches in length. We paddled all around this lake fishing. We laughed and talked about the wonders of this place. It seemed to us no one had ever fished this spot before. It was exciting and awesome to catch one after another as fast as we could bait the hook with another egg.

We each had our limit by the time we circled back to our launch point. There was no good place to clean fish on the shore. It was brushy and no beach. I asked my dad if he would like to come back the next day, and he was excited about the idea. I left the canoe in the brush by the lake and packed out the bag of fish. We made it back to the station wagon and back home for a fish cleaning job. We ate a mess of fish for supper and froze the rest for Dad to take back to Pennsylvania.

The next day was cloudy with off-and-on drizzles, but with the anticipation of a good catch, who is going to stay home? August can be a rainy time in Alaska, with July probably our best month for weather. The next day we drove out Swanson River Road and turned on Swan Lake Road to our parking spot. What a relief to be able to walk into the lake with a small pack and fishing poles. The canoe was right where we left it, so we got into it and paddled around to where this lake fed through a channel into the next larger lake. We experienced the same hungry fish that just couldn't wait to devour one of our bright red salmon eggs. We would catch a fish at every cast if an egg stayed on, and if not, another was put in its place. They were real fighters and often we would lose them before we got them into the boat. Our biggest that day was seventeen inches, and Dad was proud of that pretty rainbow trout.

It was Saturday, and the number of fisherman in this wilderness remained just us two. We didn't even make it all the way around this lake before we had our limit and had to quit. It was only mid-afternoon. This trip out would be a bigger challenge for both of us because we had the canoe to pack and also the fish and the gear. I was able to pack the canoe and tie the oars up underneath and Dad packed the fish and the rods. We had our fill of fishing for the small ones, and Dad wanted to get some salmon to take home.

The next week we set out to catch some reds. I was sorry my folks waited till August to come and missed out on the kings and a lot of the reds. We did catch a few reds in the Kenai at the mouth of the Moose River.

The next day I decided to go up toward Cooper Landing and the Russian River. In 1966 you didn't see fisherman at the mouth of the Russian River or the shoulder-to-shoulder fishermen as you do now. There is a little eddy along the highway before you get to Russian River where fish would rest on their way to spawn. That day there were a lot of them in this pool, and we were able to catch three fish each in short while. Red salmon do not strike or bite at bait like kings and silvers. They are mostly snagged as your line crosses the water just off of the bottom. As you are reeling from upstream and with weighted line bouncing along the bottom, with short jerks you snag a fish going up river. Only those caught in the mouth can be kept. The regulations have changed so much over the years and have gotten so difficult that the joke is now you will soon have to lasso them without hook or bait.

My folks had a great time in Alaska, and my Dad was able to freeze about seventy pounds of fish to take back to Altoona, Pennsylvania. They invited their friends from church to a big cookout, and the reports from that event were exciting.

Camp black bear

CHAPTER 20

Camp Black Bear

As I mentioned before, the Lord has been extremely good to my family in providing our every need as He promised in Philippians 4:19 KJV. With a missionary salary of four hundred dollars per month for many years, it was necessary to hunt and fish and live on Alaska bounty. I hunted and we ate twenty-two moose, fifteen caribou, three black bear, a goat, and lots of fish.

I thought every year I would probably be able to get my moose on the camp's 194-acre property, but it never happened. One moose season when I was on special assignment in the *lower forty-eight*, my neighbor shot a young bull in my front yard.

We did have a six-foot black bear hanging around our lodge. One evening the dogs barked as the bear worked his way from one house to another. The bear left our garbage can by the lodge because he was spooked and went on over to the neighbor's about a quarter mile away. I thought he would be back, so I propped the upstairs lodge dorm door open a crack and watched out the guest room window. I watched for a good ninety minutes. He didn't return where I could see him. When I checked out the back door of the lodge, there he was looking down into the garbage barrel. I quietly stuck the barrel of my rifle out through the door crack as he stood up and turned sideways. I shot him through both lungs, and he still ran probably seventy-five feet before he fell on the side bank of the hill. My boys were told to stay in the house, but after the shot they came running. The bear rug hung on my family room wall until we lost our home to fire in 2004. Alaskan black bears, of all the bears of North America, I am told, have a gleaming shine to their coat that is more noticeable than other black bear.

CHAPTER 21

The Last Moose

In 1987, at age fifty-six, I began to feel my days of great moose adventures should be slowing down, if not coming to a halt. But Verlin Hoffman, my maintenance supervisor at Solid Rock, asked me if I wanted to go moose hunting with him. He had hunted on Kalgin Island two years before and had gotten a moose. It was open for a cow or bull. I needed moose, but I didn't really have time to be off on a wild moose chase that didn't pan out. I told Verlin to go ahead with arrangements for a flight over to the island and back. If all worked out, I would know the Lord had a moose for us. He proceeded with the arrangements.

Verlin had arranged for Mark Gaede to take us over and for a bush pilot with a Cessna 180 with beach tires to bring us and the moose back. The day we were to go we had a small retreat at camp. I went over to check the dining hall at 11:15 because most of my staff were on vacation, and we hired a cook to prepare the food. One of our staff and a teen boy volunteered to help. I got to the dining hall and no tables were set. I asked where the help was, and the cook said the teen had gotten ill and the staff member took him home. I set all the tables in time for the meal and after began to clean up. My assistant, Ted McKenney, came in and said, "Bert, I thought you were going hunting."

I said, "Only if everything works out to go." He said he would clean up and that I should go as planned.

I picked up Verlin and off we went to Gaede's homestead airstrip. We arrived and Mark came out and said, "Verlin, the tide is going to change, and I have two guys to get out to Kalgin before you. I don't think I have time to get both groups out."

I was totally relaxed and said, "Hey, Mark, no problem. We only want to go if it all works out." Just then Dr. Gaede, Mark's dad, came out of the hangar and said, "I was going caribou hunting down at Lake Iliamna, but it is fogged in. Verlin, I'll take you over first and come back and get Bert."

It all worked out well, and when Doc took me over and landed on the beach, Verlin was up on the bank waving at me. When I got up there, he had the tent set up. "Well," I said, "Verlin, here we are, so I know the Lord has a moose for us."

You see, this is the way I prayed to the Lord. "Lord, I don't want to waste several days hunting and not get a moose. Keep us off that island unless you have a moose for us."

We still had a couple of hours of daylight and decided to do some glassing. I told Verlin to lead the way because he knew the territory. The island is very swampy with two large lakes, one in the south and one on the north end. Verlin started out the trail from our camp, and shortly we came to a moss hummock where two hunters were glassing the swamp ahead. We waved and moved on about a quarter mile. The same thing: two hunters on a knoll looking for moose.

Verlin said to me, "This is ridiculous. I have never seen this many hunters."

We went back to camp, got our mattresses blown up and sleeping bags in order, built a nice fire, and sat around and talked. This was Monday evening, and our pickup plane was due Thursday at 2:00 p.m. We went to bed and got up before it was light and had our breakfast so we could head out at dawn. This is the first time I hunted with hip boots, and it was no fun in this terrain.

We trudged across a big swamp to the northwest of our camp and came out on a dry plateau with trees and clumps of brush. We would sit, rest, and glass the open spots. We ate our lunch about noon and walked on through the area. We heard a shot not too far from us, then a second. We made our way toward the shots and came upon a guy who shot a small cow moose at the edge of a swamp.

The rest of the day was quiet and of no consequences, so we went back to camp and had our supper. The next day we went south on the island and exhausted ourselves walking through swamps. We heard a *swoosh, swoosh*, like moose walking through water and, as we watched, here came a hunter plodding along. Later that day we heard shots to the north end of the island, and a few hours later a helicopter flew over and circled about a mile away. We found out after we got home that a hunter from the Russian village near Anchor Point shot another hunter who was sitting, leaning against a tree. He apparently didn't have any orange on him, but he certainly was not a moose. They were not hunting together, but still there was no excuse. The rest of the day was uneventful, and we ended up back at camp. Now Tuesday was history. I still was trusting the Lord that He had a moose for us, but I knew it had to be soon.

After our early supper I said, "Verlin, I'm going to leave this up to your judgment what we should do." He suggested we go back over to the big swamp where we had been for our last full day. I suggested we just take our sleeping bag, food, and plastic to put under and over us if it rained, and not move our camp. He agreed, and since we had eaten, we decided to go and have time to glass the area before dark and perhaps get our moose. We had two large swamps to go through with a little terra firma between and on each end. It was a good three-quarters of a mile from our tent camp to this big swamp. We arrived in time to glass the area. Out in front beyond the trees, at the edge of the swamp, you could see a half mile in two to three directions. The swamp came around to the right of the table of land where we were going to sleep. That area to the right caved in on both sides to a point where the water stopped and a brushy moose trail started. Nothing happened before dark, so we set up our sleeping gear and plastic for the night. I was exhausted and slept like a dead man.

Evidently not so for Verlin, because very early before it was light, he said there was a moose snorting and moving around close to our spot. It had to be a bull, probably looking for a cow, because it was getting close to rutting time in late August. We tied up the gear after eating some cold food. We forgot about a fire, which would only alert a moose, and we both took our battle stations. Verlin took the big swamp in front, and I went to the narrow right side where the trail came to the lake. I was sitting on a deadfall log right at the edge of the swamp, pretty much in the open, so I couldn't move. I couldn't see Verlin because of the brush around the swamp, and he was to my left and in front of the camp spot. We heard two shots at about 9:30. Ten-thirty came and went, then 11:30. Moose usually lay down in the middle of the day or mid-afternoon. I began to pray, "Lord, I know you have a moose for us, but if you don't show us soon, we won't have time to pack it out."

It wasn't more than fifteen minutes when I heard a *slosh, slosh* in the narrow swamp to my right, and I thought, *Oh great, another hunter.* Then the noise changed to a hoof sound on dirt as he left the swamp to the trail. As I watched, the sound was across from me coming to the swamp. I spotted a nice bull moose with a thirty-seven-inch rack come to the edge of the swamp and stop. I didn't dare move. He looked right at me but didn't distinguish danger. He was standing broadside at 100 to 125 feet. He seemed to be debating as to whether he should go across that open swamp. I very slowly raised up my rifle, clicked off the safety, aimed for his hump behind his neck, and squeezed—but the trigger wasn't engaged. I was sick. I had reloads and thought maybe I had a bad one. I slowly let my gun down, operated the bolt a little, closed it, and put the bolt down. As I raised my rifle, he saw me moving and was getting nervous, but I shot before he could run. He decided instantly he was not going across the swamp.

He turned around toward the trail, and I put another shot in the hump on his right side and he collapsed in a pile.

When Verlin heard the shots, he came running around from my left through the swamp. The water flying up off of his boots made a circle of water like a paddle boat. I wished for a movie camera. He was yelling, "He may not be dead. They can get up and run." Verlin administered the final shot to the head. The Lord rewarded our faith in the nick of time.

You have heard of buffalo skinners. Well, Verlin is a moose skinner, and he can dress out a moose faster than anyone I know. Solid Rock Bible

Camp was on the *road kill* list. When we got a call to get a moose killed on the highway, Verlin was out there and back in a couple of hours. I went with him several times. He also butchered moose for needy families of the area. I wouldn't want to guess how many he has dressed out.

Well, the way his knife was already flying, I decided to go the few yards to our sleeping spot, get down, and thank the Lord for His goodness and faithfulness. Then I went back to help. We got the moose dressed out, cut up, and on our pack boards for our first pack out to our tent camp. Verlin consented to pack the hindquarters, and I would take the front shoulders, one at a time, of course. He was fifteen years younger, so it was nice of him, because the front shoulders had to be about ninety pounds.

After three packs each, we had all the moose and gear back at our tent camp, staggering through those two large swamps to get there. It was late evening of our last night, and we hung up the meat to cool overnight. The next morning we had everything packed down to the beach by ten, waiting for our plane. There were berries everywhere—salmon berries and blueberries that we knew our wives would appreciate. So we trudged back up on the bank and began to pick. It was about two in the afternoon when our plane arrived, and we each had a gallon of berries.

We loaded the moose first, then our gear, and then ourselves. The tide was coming in, and we had no time to waste. There was a stream on the south beach, and up the beach to the north was a large tree embedded in the sand. So our pilot got as close to the stream as he could, held the brakes, revved up the engine, and tore up the beach heading toward the tree, hoping our weight would not be too much to clear. It looked like we cleared it by at least ten feet, and we were off over Cook Inlet and back to Soldotna and the Gaede Eighty.

CHAPTER 22

Down the Kenai River in a Canoe

In June 1975, Tim and Kim Hiner came to Alaska to be counselors at Solid Rock. Tim was an avid fisherman, and every Saturday he took his canoe down the Kenai River, launching at Moose River. He learned the river that summer and caught lots of fish of every variety. Tim later became a guide on the river and for years has been known among the best. I took one trip with Tim that first summer and filmed our exciting catches from one spot to another. We caught trout, dollies, and salmon as we floated the Kenai River.

Every summer Tim knew my time was limited for going fishing, and he would call me the night before if he had an empty seat in the boat. I would make arrangements to be gone for the next morning. I always got my limit because Tim knew where the fish were, and the Lord knew my need.

One June day Tim invited me, my son Steve, and Vince Spady to go king salmon fishing. We were a mile or two above the Soldotna Bridge. We drifted down the river, our line weights bouncing along the bottom of the river when *bang*, a huge king salmon hit my salmon eggs and hook. I let him take it and then sank the hook as I was instructed, and away that king went upstream. Tim fired up the motor, and when I had slack, I would reel in as fast as I could, and then zing went the line out as the fish tugged. After forty minutes that seemed an eternity, the king was tiring out. I got him up alongside the boat, and Tim netted him. We found out later he weighed sixty pounds.

We went back to our drifting spot and started again. When we drifted to a certain spot Tim would yell, "Pull up," and we would all reel in because of brush sweepers from the bank hanging over in the water. We didn't want to get snagged in them. After a few drifts, my son Steve nailed a big king. Steve was fourteen years old, tall, and well-built for his age. In high school basketball, he set two school records. Steve caught his fish, and it was a monster weighing fifty-nine pounds. He landed it in a shorter time than his dad. Later on, Tim caught his king, and when we got it in the boat, he bopped it on the head with a fish bopper, which looks like a sawed-off baseball bat. Fish that size can be dangerous flopping around in a boat.

Things got awful quiet for quite a time. We made several floats, and I started to pray that the Lord would give Vince his fish. That would limit out the boat. Tim said we were only going to make a couple more passes and still no fish for Vince. Tim announced we were making our last pass, and I began to pray out loud, "Please, Lord, give Vince a king and limit out our boat." I looked and could see the sweepers coming up as we floated down river. "Lord, please give Vince a fish," and *bang*, a big king hit Vince's line and took off. Tim was only seconds from calling for us to pull up. Vince hung on to that king and fought it as Tim maneuvered the boat. He brought it up alongside; Tim netted it and dragged it in the boat for the bop on the head. We were rejoicing and praising the Lord for answered prayer. We got back to Centennial Park where we had launched, cleaned our fish, and gave the eggs to Tim for his bait. We cleaned up the boat, and Steve and I loaded our kings in the station wagon and bid farewell with much thanks.

We drove over to the drug store and weighed our fish on the outside scale. Mine was sixty pounds and Steve's was fifty-nine pounds. Two guys pulled up in a pickup with their kings, and they were fifty-eight and fifty-seven and a half pounds. We must have caught four fish that were in the same grade in school to be that close.

Every summer, Tom, a friend of Tim's, would come to visit, and Tim invited me to go along silver salmon fishing. It was in August. His family was along for an outing. He wanted to be right at the spot he had picked by six in the morning and ready to fish. We pulled in above the mud banks down river. The tide was coming in, and Tim anchored in the channel at a precise spot known to him. In a short while there were boats lined up behind us and five or six on down the river from us. As always, I prayed for the Lord to provide fish, especially silvers, some of which I would smoke in our smoker. We all baited up with Tim's special salmon egg formula and began to fish. It wasn't five minutes before the first fish was on the line, jumping and flopping for its life. We would all pull up our lines if the fish was on our side. Otherwise we would keep on fishing. We would help the fisherman who had the fish on his or her line, net it, and bring it into the boat. It would be bonked and marked on the tail with a notch to identify who caught it. In a short while, we had two and once three fish on lines at the same time. The other boats were looking at us, because we were catching all the fish. They wanted to float into our spot when we pulled up anchor and moved out.

That's exactly what happened, and we went up river to the island near Beaver Creek and pulled the boat up on the shore. We strung all the fish on a pole and held them up for pictures of us, the fish, and Tim's boat. The picture tells the rest of the story. Well, not quite, because when we finished taking pictures, we looked around and there were four boats anchored in the river getting ready to fish because they thought that's where we were fishing. They never asked, and we never let on. The total time it took for us to catch our limit of fish was one hour and forty-five minutes.

Bert and Steve with 60 and 61 pound King salmon

CHAPTER 23

A Trophy Rainbow

In the late nineties Tim called me and asked if I would like to go late silver salmon fishing. I never went with Tim that I didn't get fish, and usually it was my limit. My answer was a resounding *yes* for early the next morning, October 10. We left Centennial Park launch around six in the morning and headed down the river. The temperature hovered at twenty-five, and at thirty miles per hour it was severely cold. With the open boat at that speed, it was well below zero degrees chill factor. I was glad when we finally stopped above Beaver Creek and anchored in Tim's perfect selected spot. We had been fishing for about thirty minutes when I got a strike. The fish jumped out of the water and Tim got a good look at it, but I couldn't see because he was sitting in front of the motor and blocked my view. Excited, Tim said, "Bert, you've got a terrific fish. Better than any silver or a king." I wondered what in the world that would be. I fought that baby for ten to fifteen minutes, drag going out singing and then pumping him my way when he let up. Finally I brought the fish up to the boat, and Tim netted him and brought him into the boat. Tim said, "Bert, look, you have a beautiful trophy rainbow trout." It measured thirty and a half inches and weighed eleven pounds. I was flabbergasted. Tim has seen and caught some twenty-eight to twenty-nine inches, but never this big. What was great is the fact its fins were in excellent condition with no damage.

Tim said, "You are going to have to get this baby mounted."

I said, "Yeah, but not on my salary." I knew about what it cost.

It was really cold, and we didn't get a strike for quite a while, so we headed back to the ramp. When we got back to Tim's home, Kim came out and said, "Well, what great catch did Bert make today?" She knew how the Lord always answered prayer for me in a special way. Tim showed her the huge rainbow trout, and she said immediately, "You have got to get this fish mounted." I asked what it would cost. Kim said, "If you want it mounted, I will prepare it for the taxidermist for free." She usually was paid thirty-five dollars for a fish this size. She said, "It would be one hundred twenty dollars when you take it to the taxidermist. After about six months, when it is finished, you pay the other one hundred twenty dollars."

"I appreciate your offer, but I don't know." Then I realized I had a birthday coming up on October 30, and possibly my wife Donna would consent to the down payment for my birthday. She did consent, and my fish was prepared and taken to the taxidermist. The best part is you get to eat that delicious meat, look at the mount, and remember that exciting day and how good God was to provide us with such wonderful creatures to enjoy.

CHAPTER 24

Hairy Fish

My boys were ten years apart, which made it very difficult to take them both hunting at the same time. Scott, my oldest, had come home from two years at college in Pennsylvania. He was home working the summer of 1976 and wanted to go moose hunting again with Dad and brother, Steve, who was a big ten year old, tall and husky. He worked with the horses at Solid Rock and knew how to do it all as a wrangler's helper. We took Babe and Winky, a one-eyed horse that could see and smell moose better than two horses. I don't remember what other horse we took for Scott to ride. You can bet we checked the belly strap on this trip.

There was nothing different about the preparation and trip back up to our campsite on Fuller Lake Trail—except it was five years later and gorgeous as usual with the birch leaves now turning a bright yellow and the aspen turning a yellow orange. All that was mixed into the beautiful green of the spruce growing along the far side of the lake with the low ground cover mixed with red and green. It was a picture I can't describe in words, but I still can see it in my mind's eye after all these years and after all those hunting trips.

We crossed the little creek at the far end of Fuller Lake, past the big, rounded rock tables, and then we could see our camping spot, which was empty as always. It wasn't until the eighties that I saw other hunters in the area, and that's when I decided to go elsewhere.

We set up camp and glassed the hillside as we always did in the evening. We saw a cow or two over that vast area of green fields surrounded by alder patches. That evening we sat at the fire that felt so good because the evenings were now getting down into the mid-forties and lower. My boys loved hot chocolate, so instead of coffee, I enjoyed a cup with them as we talked, and I shared hunting stories. In the morning, after a good breakfast of scrambled eggs, bacon, a cold glass of orange juice plus hot chocolate, we began glassing the hills.

I decided to walk up the trail along the creek and Steve wanted to go along, but Scott decided to stay behind and lay on his sleeping bag in the tent till we came back. Steve and I walked about quarter mile and climbed up on the side of the mountain so we could get a better view. We could see the camp below us at about two hundred feet. As we glassed with the binoculars, a big cow moose and her calf came up the trail beyond our camp, and she was heading right for our tent. We yelled at Scott that moose were coming toward him. He came out, looked up at us, and then dove into the tent just before the moose went by on the trail, down across the creek, and into the thick woods. Steve and I almost fell off of the cliff laughing when Scott finally came out shaking and muttering. We told him later, "That will teach you to stay behind in the comfort of your sleeping bag."

We were looking down on the trail and ahead over the trail's ridge, when a huge bull moose, a good seventy-five to a hundred yards away, crossed the trail from right to left. His rack was in the high fifties to low sixties range, and we only saw him for four to five seconds as he crossed and out of view. Steve and I clambered down off the side of the mountain to the trail and headed toward where we saw the moose. We only had one gun, and I wanted Steve to be able to get his moose, so I positioned him in a clump of trees where he could see up and down the creek bed. I went beyond where we saw the moose and carefully circled around, stopping and listening, hoping the moose would move toward Steve who was upstream. I heard the moose once crack sticks with his hooves behind me to the left. Cautiously I made my way toward Steve's position, but we never did see that big bull again. We figured he circled in the brush behind Steve and disappeared.

We walked back to camp and decided to go over to Dyke Creek, which was two valleys farther in from our camp. My concern was finding my way through that swamp without Bob, who also had difficulty but could find it. We packed up our camp and gear, and I led the way out the trail that goes about two miles and then disappears. Shortly we came to the swampy bog, and I tried to get around it at the edge of the alders, but they grow downhill and push right at you out over the swamp. Winky took two steps, and he barely pulled loose from the mud.

I didn't want to lose a horse. I decided we would go right up over the mountain, following the moose trails through the alder patches. We found a rough trail, and I started up, leading my horse from one alder patch to another. When you got into a clearing in the tall grass, you had to find the best moose trail through the alders and on up the mountain. It was steep, and the alders would catch on our pack, and the horses would whinny and snort but kept on following. We would rest in the meadow and decide if the moose trail led through the alder. We were getting exhausted, and the horses were panting. We finally got to the top of the mountain and had to figure out how to get down into Dyke Creek.

Going up, we could see across the grass and up the mountain to where the openings were through the alder. Now, going down the mountain, the alder blocked our view and we couldn't see the openings. Scott would climb a tree and look on top of the alder and see where the opening went through to the next field. This time Scott led the way and pointed out the openings. The only thing that was better going down was the fact it wasn't climbing, but also the alder were growing away from us down the mountain instead of pointing at us. Therefore the horses and pack slid through much easier. Scott would climb another tree and see the opening into the next field and out. We finally made it out of the last alder patch and down to the creek. The whole *over the mountain* experience took a good three hours. And lo and behold, there was the trail that headed back to the swamp we circumvented.

We came out just about a quarter mile from where Bob and I camped before on two occasions. It was late afternoon on our second day, so we decided to set up camp and grab a bite to eat. I started lunch after we all pitched in to build a fire on the stony creek side. Scott and Steve were excited to see salmon spawning this far upstream in the mountains. Dyke Creek was about eight to ten feet wide there, and in a short time I looked at the boys running up and down the creek in their shorts with sticks they had made into spears to try and stick a fish. The fish were darting all around as they yelled and plunged their spears into the water to no avail.

All at once Scott yelled, "Look at that hairy fish." It was a muskrat they had scared out from under the creek bank. It took off upstream. When I told Scott that furry fish was a muskrat, we all started laughing uncontrollably. This may be the reason we never did see another bull moose, even though we hunted the rest of the day. They sure knew where we were.

I wish I could show you a panoramic view with the five-hundred-foot-high hills rising up on each side of us and Dyke Creek flowing out of the mountain straight ahead. We rode our horses up to the top and looked out over Cooper Landing in the distance and beautiful Kenai Lake trailing beyond. We just sat up there and drank in the beauty of God's great creation so pure and clean and unmolested.

After a great night of camping by Dyke Creek, we glassed the hills and mountains around the alder patches but didn't spot any bull that morning. We decided to pack up camp and head back to our first camp at the end of Fuller Lake. The trail back out led through the swamp and trees. When coming the other way, for some reason it is difficult to find. I remember one time Bob put toilet paper on the trees and brush to mark the trail, knowing the rain would wash it away and no one else would be able to find it. We made it back and set up the tent and built a nice fire.

The boys were sitting around the fire drinking some hot chocolate, and I had spread out my sleeping bag to take a short nap. I was lying there thinking of the privilege as a dad to have both of my boys together on such a beautiful campout. I closed my eyes and went over our trip with the horses going up through those alder patches, trying to get over the mountain, and wondered what someone would have thought if they had seen us in such a location with horses. Then I thought of the boys in the creek shouting and jumping trying to spear a fish and the hairy one. By now it was too much, and I started to chuckle. The laugh got louder and louder till both Scott and Stephen came into the tent to see what was Dad's problem. After trying to explain between snickers, they caught on and again we all had a good laugh.

Our location for camping and spotting moose was excellent, and we watched and spotted till it was dark. There was definitely a change in the success of getting a moose over the past fifteen years. Through I only encountered other hunters on two occasions, there were definitely more hunters and moose taken out of this area than in the past. We had a great evening around the campfire, just talking about our experiences, and ended the evening with a devotional time and thanks to the Lord for a great trip.

The next morning after glassing the hills, we packed up our gear and horses for the trip out and down the trail. This is the first hunt I ever came up empty without game, but I was not disappointed because the time with my boys was of great importance and less work without a moose.

Bert and Dad Porte on 1992 fishing trip.

Fishing the Kenai with guide Tim Hiner

Cook Inlet and Mt Redoubt

CHAPTER 25

Halibut Trip to Homer

I've gone halibut fishing several times, and the biggest I ever caught was sixty pounds to match my king salmon. Verlin Hoffman planned a trip for a halibut charter in Homer. He asked if I wanted to go along with him and Andrew, his son. We needed halibut for our freezer, and everyone loves to eat mouthwatering halibut.

It's amazing the way the Lord worked, but for some reason the charter we were going to go on was cancelled, so we ended up going with another charter. We arrived at the dock promptly at seven in the morning, but the other three members who were from Southeast Alaska had not arrived. I struck up a conversation with the captain, explaining that the three of us were Christians and that we needed fish for the winter and that God has always been faithful to provide for us. We had also prayed about this trip for His direction. The captain looked at me and said, "Then you want to go where the big ones are?" and I agreed.

The group finally all arrived. Soon we were headed out around the Homer Spit, which is the second largest land spit in the world, five miles in length, jutting out into Kachemak Bay. I stood up front with the captain and chatted about things in general and shared my testimony with him. We headed straight toward Mount Augustine, which is a volcanic mountain that juts right up out of the ocean on the Alaska Peninsula.

We traveled about two hours out of Homer near the end of the Kenai Peninsula. The captain anchored the boat above a mound about thirty feet high as he described it to me. He lowered the anchor and proceeded to prepare each rod for us, baiting the large hook with a good size piece of herring. We had been fishing for ten minutes, and Verlin had a strike. It was a good one.

When a halibut takes the bait and hook and it sinks into his mouth, he'll fight to stay on the bottom. Being a wide, flat fish, it is hard to get them up to the top. Often you get them up most of the way, and down they go again, and you can't hold those big ones. On a previous trip, I got a sixty pounder up to the surface and was bringing it close to the boat. The captain shot it in the head to get it safely on board, but his shot grazed the fish's head and down to the bottom he went again. This time the fish was not wanting to cooperate at all. It took me twenty minutes to pump and reel him back up, and this time the shot was good.

On this trip, Verlin, after quite a while, got his to the surface, and the captain shot it in the head twice. He then gaffed it with a long pole gaff, and it took three guys to pull it into the boat, still flopping. They are very dangerous and can break your leg with that powerful tail. This fish weighed one hundred-eighty pounds and had to be tied to the boat rail. After the excitement died down, it wasn't long before Andrew hooked into a huge halibut. He worked and worked till it broke the surface and was reeled into a position to shoot it. Then it was pulled on board and tied to the rail.

I was next and latched onto a ninety-pound halibut. It took me as long to bring it up as it did Verlin and Andrew with their fishes twice as big. The arthritis in my shoulders let me know it was a struggle. It was shot, gaffed, and pulled over to the rail. This was all happening within a short period of time, and the captain was really excited to see us so happy. I later caught a thirty pounder. The guys from Southeast caught a hundred-thirty, three twenty-to-thirty, and two fifty-to-sixty pounders, for a total of eleven fish in several hours. We each had all the fish we wanted and needed, so we prepared the deck and pulled the anchor.

The captain started the engine and headed back to the Homer small boat harbor. I was glad it was not low tide because the floating walkways are really steep and a long way up. The tide was about halfway. So it was easier to get the huge fish up to the truck to load. We all took our own vehicles back to the charter office and hung up the fish for the story picture. The captain and his helper cut up each fish in large chunks and put them in separate bags for the fisherman. Verlin, Andrew, and I had a large tub and buckets for our fish.

The interesting conversation on the way back was when the captain said to me, "Bert, in all the years I have had a charter business, I have never seen this many big fish caught in such a short time. Prayer must work." That's why I penned this book, *Hunting and Fishing by Faith*. The spiritual part of seeking men, women, boys, and girls for Christ is through prayer and the Word of God. Yet, hunting game, fishing, and trusting the Lord for His provision are more than fun. It is exciting to see His faithfulness.

CHAPTER 26

Once in a Lifetime Experience

Ted Sires, a commercial fisherman, served on Solid Rock Bible Camp's Board of Directors. He owned a fifty-two-foot wooden boat named the *Sword*. He was one of two trawlers in the whole Gulf of Alaska. They fished for premature king salmon, which were caught with hooks in the mouth on imitation fluorescent squid. It was a limited fishery for a Seward broker who sold to the Jewish kosher market in New York. They also caught halibut, which helped with the boat expenses.

Ted had taken out two other missionaries on previous trips, who would help with the catch, pay for their license, and reap a good supply of halibut for their winter's food. One missionary, whom I will not identify, went on the trip before me, and the weather was a bit rough. The first morning Ted called for him to come up for breakfast, but he didn't come. After a while, Ted looked down the ladder and saw him kneeling at this bunk and thought he was having a rather long prayer time—later to discover the missionary was throwing up and was at the dry heaves stage, wishing he would die.

I assured Ted I was okay about seasickness and shouldn't have any problem. We left out of Seward, Alaska, one mid-October day before noon with a crew of three: Ted, me, and the cook, Mr. Hasty. This was the latest fall trip Ted had ever taken, and we didn't anticipate such stormy weather. Our goal was Middleton Island, which was approximately a hundred thirty miles in a direct line, but on the way we checked at Montague Island and a few old abandoned villages. December 21st is the shortest day of the year with five and one-half hours of daylight, which makes it dark by three-thirty in the afternoon. So this being mid-October, it would be dark by about four-thirty.

Ted put the boat on automatic pilot and told me he wanted to get some rest if I wasn't sleepy. I assured him I was wide awake. He said my biggest job was to watch out for logs or dangerous floaters that could get in the prop and cripple us by shearing a pin or other damage. We only had one diesel engine, and it was imperative to keep it going. Also I was told we would come up on large floats of Japanese or Russian ships and to watch we didn't run into one.

It was now getting dark, and Ted put on the running lights and the flood lights to light up the water on each side of the boat. He told me to let the boat run, and if I had to make a turn or had trouble, wake him because he wanted to stay on course.

Maximum speed with ideal conditions is about fourteen knots, and we were probably closer to ten to twelve knots. At that speed, we would be at our fishing grounds the next morning at daylight. Several hours went by as I stood at the wheel watching from left to right, realizing the responsibility that was on me. The cook was below in his bunk for the night, and Ted was behind me to my left on the couch sleeping away. About two in the morning, I saw lights in the distance, and there were at least twenty of them. We kept getting closer and closer. After a while, one's eyes play tricks on you, and you think you are closer then you really are. Off to my starboard was a huge fishing boat, lit up like a Christmas tree, and all of those little boats were charging toward her to deposit their catch of the day.

It was a huge Japanese processing cannery freezer ship. This was in the early 1980s, and they were close to being inside our Alaska boundary waters.

The large ship drags a net with chainlike bottom edge and scoops everything from trash, fish, clams, halibut, crab, and anything that is sea life into the net. They haul it up and process it for the insatiable appetite of the Orient for seafood.

I passed all the boats with the closest probably a quarter mile away and continued with running lights through the darkness. Within two hours, I came across another flotilla. It was amazing to me to see so many boats in a few hours in such a vast area the Gulf of Alaska. I had been reading a few months earlier in *Reader's Digest* about there being still some World War II floating mines in the seas of the world. This must have been on my mind. An hour or so later, the running lights to my left shown on a large round floating object that looked like spikes all over the circumference. No doubt it was a mine. I immediately called to the captain and pointed out the floating mine. Much to my surprise, he grabbed a long-handled net after idling down the engine and netted the sphere the first try. I grabbed the back of the long handle and helped pull it on board, knowing by then it couldn't be a mine or Ted would not be bringing it on board. Immediately I recognized it as a very large glass Japanese float that still had its netting woven around it, covered with black and brown barnacles that gave it its hobnail mine look.

I thought, *Am I lucky for that find.* They were worth a couple hundred bucks and are very rare because plastic took over years ago for float lines on nets. Later I saw that huge float all cleaned up sitting in Ted's living room.

Ted throttled back up, checked our course, and then went back to the sack. The night became much longer with nothing exciting except the responsibility to watch for any logs or large debris. Often there were the large chunks of kelp that spooked me to attention floating by on one side or the other. Morning was beginning to dawn, and light was beginning to show faintly ahead of us. Soon Captain Ted was awake and talking about breakfast, and it wasn't long until our cook came up from the lower bunk room. Breakfast was decided on, and I cast my vote for the bacon, eggs, and toast, but not without coffee first.

We had to see what the weather was going to be like in order to plan our fishing strategy. The strength of the wind determines everything, the calmer the better, especially if your duty is in the hold laying down the fish as they are cleaned. It was finally time to fish, and Ted had already decided the location. We throttled back to the trolling speed and trolled along Middleton Island's east side. The lines were baited with plastic fluorescent squid, and each long line had approximately fifteen squid. With six electric reels with lines, that amounts to ninety hooks put into operation.

It wasn't long till the poles here and there began to jiggle. The captain discerned when to reel them up because some are still biting, but also you don't want them to get off if they struggle too long. You may get one to two fish on a line or six to ten at a time, depending on the amount of fish feeding off of the island's banks. There was a mixture of fish, from halibut to king salmon and once in a while an Irish lord or stingray. I was allowed to clean halibut but not the king salmon. The king salmon had to be cleaned carefully, and not a fish scale could be damaged.

My job was almost exclusively receiving each king salmon handed down, icing their bellies with crushed ice, and stacking them in rows on their backs. When a layer was completed, the whole layer is iced and another layer started. The halibut were put in a different hold with ice thrown on them. Each day was the repeat of the former as long as the weather cooperated. Sometimes it was too rough to fish.

The fishing was not very good, and we wondered if he would make enough to pay expenses. Then the radio told us that a storm was brewing with winds picking up to twenty to thirty knots. Ted decided to head on east across the gulf toward Yakataga, which is north of Yakatat. He thought it would be better to go into Icy Bay and anchor up until the storm died down. That is exactly what we did. The other trawler and friend of Ted's was already in the bay, and they talked to each other over the radio about the weather.

Ted suggested we take the dory and go ashore and do a little moose hunting. I was all for going to shore just to get my *landlubbin'* feet back after a week and a half on the sea. As we were anchoring offshore about two hundred yards, we saw a huge brown bear come out of the brush and down to the beach. He turned and started up the beach in the direction of the glacier. When we got to shore with our rifles, we decided to follow him to see where he was going. By the size of his paw prints, we figured he was between eight and nine feet tall. He was still padding along up the beach a good half mile ahead of us, and then he went into the brush where we did not want to follow.

We walked all the way back toward the *Sword* and decided to check some shacks along the top of the beach. Ted explained that the native hunters come here during seal hunting season. They stay in the shacks, shoot seal, and clean them for their winter's meat. None of the shacks were intact. Each had a wall busted out or doors torn off their hinges. They all smelled of seal oil and who knows what else. The bears also made their rounds to get their snacks because they also like seal meat. I could just picture the scene with both man and animal competing for the seal meat. I wouldn't have wanted to be in that camp before, during, or after seal season. I'm sure those hunters had some stories to tell much better than mine!

We found a trail through the brush and decided to look for moose sign. There was very little, and it was all winter moose droppings. Maybe the bear got all the moose. It was basically too thick to hunt with no openings, so we went back and decided to row back to the boat. The rest of the day was short with darkness coming. We had a good supper, chatted, and hit the bunk.

The next morning we were all up by seven and had breakfast. The weather report was not good, with high seas and thirty-to-forty-knot winds. Another problem had developed—the wind was coming out of the glacier behind us, and the icebergs were flowing toward the mouth of the bay and were getting thicker and larger. Ted radioed the other boat, and they discussed the problem. The captain of the other boat decided to stay another day and take his fish to Yakataga. Ted said that another day with the ice blocking the bay and he may not get out at all, and the whole catch would spoil. Ted decided to work our way out of the icy bay now while we could and make a run for Seward.

We pulled anchor after warming the engine and slowly made our way through the icebergs, most of which were the size of a bathtub, and we meandered through the larger ones. I stood in the bow with a long pole and pushed those at our bow to the left or right and they would slide by as we *slo-o-o-o-wly* moved forward. We got through the Gulf and headed toward Middleton Island, hoping to find shelter on the south side of the island. Our cook was hoping to prepare a good substantial meal before we started for Seward. We saw the wind change direction and the rollers coming right at us. We had a change in food menu and ate cold sandwiches because we couldn't anchor or find shelter.

We were now at the mercy of the huge waves caused by the strong wind. Ted said we were going to make a run for it all the way to Seward. When we rounded the last point off Middleton Island, felt the full force of the wind, and saw the height of the waves, I was overwhelmed. When we were in the wave trough, the waves were more than thirty feet above us. As the wave rolled under us, we rose the thirty feet to the top as part of the wave broke over our bow, splashing up on the cabin pilothouse windows. Water leaked through onto the floor and at the cabin door; up and down we went hundreds of times. Ted looked back to make sure the fish hold lids were buttoned down good and holding. Many fishing vessel has gone down when they lost their hatch covers and the bilge filled with water.

Then Ted noticed that his tackle box had gone overboard with all of his fluorescent plastic squid that we used for bait lures. It was floating with the long line tied to the back of the boat. It was worth three or four hundred dollars, and he couldn't afford to lose it. He said he was going back to try to pull it up and into the boat.

I thought he was crazy because the waves would wash over the sides up to two feet deep and pour out the gunnels. It was easy to be washed overboard, but he went back anyway. I was praying and watching as he hung on to the rigging, and the sides, or anything he could get a grip on. He was a powerful, strong fisherman. He got the rope and began to hand walk the fish lure box hand over hand, struggling and hanging on between waves. He got the box to within ten feet of the boat but couldn't hang on and had to let it go. He struggled back to the cabin totally exhausted and collapsed on the cabin bunk. I was relieved he made it back and hoped he saw the futility of the matter.

After fifteen to twenty minutes, he firmly addressed the cook and me with a very serious conversation. He said, "I am going to go back and make another try at getting the fish lure box into the boat." I thought he was now insane, and the instruction to us proved it. He said, "Listen, you guys, if I don't make it and go overboard, just keep going. We are on autopilot; the course is set for Resurrection Bay opening to Seward. Don't try to turn or the waves will roll up like a blanket and all will be lost. Do you understand?"

Yes, but we don't understand your trying again, I thought.

Well, Ted went down the steps from the cabin and at the bottom made his way back to the stern. The farther he was away from the cabin, the more water there was to pour over the side, attacking him and trying to wash him overboard. He worked his way cautiously back to the left corner of the stern as he hung on to anything he could. He reached the rope and began to hand walk the tackle box slowly to himself hand over hand, closer and closer, from about thirty-five feet out. I prayed silently that he would have the strength for success, and the Lord honored that prayer. He lifted the box over the stern and tied it down securely. I didn't breathe normally till he made his way back into the cabin and sat down on the bunk. It was time to cheer and praise God for His goodness.

We continued to roll to the top of the waves and down into the deep troughs for another twelve or more hours. It seemed like an eternity to me. We saw the channel lights for the entrance of Resurrection Bay in the far distance, which made me feel somewhat better. My camera was up on the windowsill of the pilothouse, and the salt water did a final number on it. It never worked after that, and the film was ruined. So we have another story without pictures, but hopefully I got the picture into your minds by the writing of words.

When I read Paul's account of the storm and shipwreck in Acts 27 KJV, I know a little more about what it must have been like in that storm. We all got enough fish for the winter and paid for my license, but there was no profit on this trip for Ted. My thanks went to him with the comment, "That was a once-in-a-lifetime experience, and I never want to go through it again."

Water portage on Swan Lake Canoe System

CHAPTER 27

Miraculous
Catch of Fish

The following story is taken from *Miracle at Solid Rock, An Alaskan Adventure*, written by my wife, Donna Schultz, and me.

In the early seventies, the Swan Lake Canoe Trail System in the Kenai National Moose Range was established. The Swanson River road, fifteen miles of gravel, led to the trail head. The trail system consists of several routes with water and land portages. The wilderness camp program used the trail that began at the East Gate and led through several portages to Swan Lake, then down the Moose River to the Sterling Highway Bridge and Pederson Landing where the Moose River meets the mighty Kenai River. Solid Rock Bible Camp offered canoe camps to families, teens, and college/career campers.

The spiritual potential of wilderness became evident one summer. Two boys from England, Simon and David, had been visiting an aunt in

Anchorage when they saw our ad in the *Anchorage Times* describing a teen canoe camp. They signed up and soon made many friends. Everyone was curious about the boys with British accents.

David and Simon were assigned to paddle with me. It happened to be the day we were to *live off the land*. We had to catch trout for supper, or else. Before getting into their canoes, the campers prayed that the Lord would supply a good catch of fish. The English boys and I started across Swan Lake.

As we paddled through the clear waters, we saw a school of trout pass under our canoe, heading for the lily pads near shore. We were surprised to see so many fish! Following them, we quietly anchored among the lily pads. We caught trout as fast as we could pull them into the canoe.

In a short time, we had our limit: ten-to-eighteen inches long. With pride, our English guests showed off their contribution to the evening meal. Other campers returned with fish, and we had enough to feed everyone with some left over.

I was the Bible teacher on that trip and had been using a lesson series by Lloyd Mattson called "Christ on the Sea." The night of our trout feed, the study was about Peter, Andrew, James, John, and the miraculous catch of fish. Simon and David sat wide-eyed. That very day, they had experienced a catch of fish beyond anything they had ever imagined. The boys knew little about the Bible, but they believed they had experienced a real-life illustration of God's power to provide. As I closed the lesson, I invited the campers to receive Christ.

Living the wilderness adventure to the hilt, the boys had built a pole and brush lean-to away from the main camp site. The next morning, while pancakes and sausage were being prepared over the fire, I went to the lean-to and called them for breakfast. As they laced their hiking boots, they told me they didn't know much about God, but when they saw Him answer prayer, they believed He was real. They had never understood that God's Son, Jesus, had died for their sins. They told me they wanted to become Christians. I showed them the Scripture about salvation, and both boys prayed to receive Christ as Savior. At the campfire that evening, they told their fellow campers that they were now Christians, and that God had spoken to them through the story of Jesus and the miraculous catch of fish.

CPSIA information can be obtained
at www.ICGtesting.com
Printed in the USA
BVHW071924280921
617708BV00014B/97